Buddhism for Teens

50 MINDFULNESS ACTIVITIES, MEDITATIONS, AND STORIES TO CULTIVATE CALM AND AWARENESS

Candradasa

ROCKRIDGE
PRESS

Interior and Cover Designer: Scott Wooledge
Art Producer: Samantha Ulban
Editor: John Makowski
Production Manager: Riley Hoffman

Illustration © 2021 Carl Wiens, cover. All other images used under license Shutterstock. Author photo courtesy of Laura Horwood-Benton.

Paperback ISBN: 978-1-63878-110-3
eBook ISBN: 978-1-63878-243-8
R0

For all my niblings by family and friends!

Laura, Marco, Chiara, Luca, Lola, Rocco,

Allegra, Adelina, Mya, Ruaridh, Dominic,

Easton, Isabelle, Marina, Mícheál,

Daniel, Anoushka, Amalia, Juliet,

and Mitra

Contents

Introduction

Welcome to *Buddhism for Teens*. Thanks for picking up this book. I hope reading it will be like taking a step into a bigger universe. That the ideas, activities, stories, and meditations you find here will help you make your way through your own worlds—at home, in school, with friends, with enemies, with any challenges you're facing—today and in the years ahead.

My name is Candradasa (pronounced Chandra-dasa). It was given to me when I was ordained into the Triratna Buddhist Order and literally means "Servant of the Moon." It's always fascinating to hear what people make of *that*!

I've benefited in so many ways since I first came across meditation and Buddhism. I knew nothing about it, but I was intrigued. Was it a philosophy? A religion? Now I'd say "a way of life" comes closest.

The Buddha is said to have lived and taught in India almost 3,000 years ago—a human being, just like the rest of us. Since then, billions of people have been inspired to live out a Buddhist path of peace that's handed down from person to person, generation to generation, telling of a way out of unhappiness toward a true understanding of life. I *love* that positive connection through long history: human beings learning and sharing a tradition of deep mindfulness and deep kindness, because it works.

Of course, it's not always easy. When I'm struggling and need help, my Buddhist practice reminds me how light can shine on anyone, even in the darkest times and places, even on me. Everyone can imagine the moon. Everyone knows the dark. They are both part of life.

Sometimes I'm invited to talk with students in middle and high school. They usually ask about the mind-boggling variety of different Buddhist schools—more varieties than Ben & Jerry's—some of which flavor this book. These students also tell me that learning meditation and mindfulness, and thinking about compassionate living, has helped them, too. I think that's because wherever it goes, whatever it looks like, the Buddhist path is deeply encouraging. You really can't do it wrong! Everyone gives themselves a hard time now and again. Buddhism gives you permission not to. Awareness + kindness: it's all you need to live better.

Thanks for joining me on this path. I'm glad to have your company for however long, under the moon and sun.

How to Use This Book

Something as old as Buddhism can take a *lot* of different forms. In the 21st century, we can benefit from all that amazing, diverse history, whatever we believe or don't believe in our own lives. Buddhism's fundamental truths aren't especially religious—they are human and belong to everyone.

Buddhist philosophy focuses on learning to live more skillfully in three ways: body, speech, and mind. The idea is that if you practice paying attention to these aspects of being human, you'll be happier and enjoy better relationships. Simple! So, in this book we'll look at how Buddhist ways of seeing things can help us in our:

1. Emotional life

2. Relationship to our body

3. Mind and how we learn

4. Connection with the wider world through society

Here you'll find intriguing stories with points to think, talk, or journal about; fun indoor and outdoor activities to get your head around (we'll be mapping our lives, time traveling, and becoming Buddhist detectives); and easy-to-use meditations you can use anytime. Each chapter has its own flow, but feel free to jump around! You might decide to start with a calming meditation on your breathing before trying one on building positive emotions. You might want to read the whole book from cover to cover, see which bits ring a bell in your own life, and then dive back in.

When people asked for life teachings, the Buddha offered some general advice:

- If someone tells you they know the truth, don't just take their word for it. Test things out in your own experience, *"the way a goldsmith tests gold."*

- Find people you trust and look up to, and listen to their perspective.

If they were still curious, they would receive this simple invitation: *"Come and see!"*

That's a great place to start with this book. A whole world awaits you.

CHAPTER 1

Your Best Emotional Life

Human beings are magical creatures. We have amazing bodies of so many different kinds. We have super-developed brains, finely tuned senses—and they all work together. We can just think of someone we love who's far away, and our skin prickles, our heart beats faster—it's like they're right there with us.

Our bodies, minds, and hearts are affected by *everything*. And sometimes it's emotionally overwhelming! Social media, school pressures, bullying, bad news in the world, worries about the future of our planet—every day we are pulled in a million directions by thoughts, feelings, pictures, words: our own and other people's. How can we even cope, taking in so much information? How can we work with anxiety and learn to live well?

The good news is these aren't new problems. In this chapter we'll explore some helpful strategies Buddhism has come up with. Time to live your best emotional life.

Finding Your Way in the Dark of the Night

The prince was unhappy. Not Disney-prince unhappy because no true love had turned up. Just discontented. *Something* was nagging at him.

He knew, on the face of it, there wasn't much to be unhappy about: he was a rich kid, the son of a king. But whoever you are, sadness happens, and it's hard to live with.

His father saw this and smelled trouble. So he spoiled the prince, kept him away from any hint of normal life and everyday troubles. It didn't work. The prince got even more unhappy. He knew he wasn't seeing the real world. He felt strongly that the truth of life was out there, if he could only find it . . .

Eventually, the prince slipped out of the palace in disguise one day. And what a day that was. Walking the streets of the city, seeing people living their lives, often struggling, sometimes poor, in pain, sick, dying, even dead. It was almost impossible to take in for someone who, the story says, had only ever seen the inside of the palace and its gardens. When he snuck back home that evening, he was reeling.

One intriguing thing stayed with him, though: He'd met a spiritual wanderer on the road. This was the most peaceful-looking person he'd ever seen. Wearing a simple robe, half rags, really, dyed by the red earth, and carrying a bowl to ask for a little food from passersby. You'd think he'd be miserable! But on the contrary, his face was calm and his manner composed. It blew the prince's mind. This beggar had nothing, yet seemed happy. Whereas he, a prince, had everything, but felt totally wretched.

The prince made up his mind: He would go on a quest to learn the meaning of existence and the way to genuine happiness. But first he'd need to escape the palace and his parents. So he hatched a plan.

In the darkest part of the night, he slipped past the guards and rode out silently on horseback. He knew he'd soon be missed and they'd come looking for him—he had to disappear. Once clear of the city, he stopped and sent his horse back toward the palace. Then, taking his sword, he cut off his princely hair, determined to make himself unrecognizable.

At the edge of the forest, he met a homeless man. The prince asked if he'd like to swap clothes: his rich robes for the man's muddy rags, very like the ones he'd seen on the wanderer. The man was delighted to trade.

And now the prince really was like a different person, at least on the outside. Messed up, but a little happier.

He took one last look at the way he'd come, and headed deeper down the forest path.

Think Points

One day, we all have to leave home and start out on our own. Wherever we go, we can't avoid suffering. But we can learn to notice what we feel and how it's affecting us. This can help us understand ourselves and make better decisions.

I. The prince decides to leave the palace to figure himself out. How do you take space for your emotional life: at home, in school, with friends?

II. What would your own mythic quest look like?

The Story of You

Throughout this book, everything you do will flow from a sense of who you are and, just as importantly, the kind of person you want to be in relationship with others.

Time to explore who you are—and your potential!

Different people learn in different ways. Feel free to answer these questions by:

- Writing things down

- Making drawings

- Talking them over with a friend

- Doing a selfie video interview

- Recording your audio thoughts

This applies to any activity you encounter in this book. Find what works best for you. It's your time, your energy, your life!

I'd suggest keeping your answers offline for now, though: no need to share this part.

1. What are your good qualities? Perhaps you have a quick mind and can usually figure stuff out for yourself. Maybe you're a generous friend or a good listener. Or you're talented at music or sports. Don't be shy or humble—go big, as many as you like, cover the walls of your room with your majesty. (JK, don't write all over your walls! Unless your parents are *that* cool.)

2. What qualities would you like to develop? It's fine to dream a little here, but it's also good to be realistic (you probably won't learn to be invisible or suddenly develop the ability to fly!).

3. What do you think those new qualities would add to your life? Why did you choose them? Maybe you feel they would make you a better person. Perhaps they are qualities you admire in someone else.

4. What are two or three aspects of your personality you'd like to let go of? These can be things that hold you back; things you struggle with or that hurt your confidence. Like always comparing yourself to other people in school. Or snapping at your sister or brother. Being specific helps keep things real and in perspective. It's important not to beat yourself up. Everyone has their weaknesses. It's what you do with them that matters. Deciding to try and let them go can be a relief. If it helps, write them on paper and throw them in the trash!

When you're done and happy with the *Story of You*, file it away for now. Come back to it at the end of the book, then do it again and see what's changed. What do you think might change?

GETTING READY TO MEDITATE

First things first: Buddhism and meditation go hand in hand. The Buddha recommended meditation for some very practical reasons. Just sitting and spending time with our thoughts and feelings can help us calm our minds, get clear about what's going on emotionally, and allow us to experience the world in new ways. In my experience, it can also be really enjoyable and restful. That's why the most important support for meditation is to be relaxed and comfortable. Here are some tips to help you get started:

- Decide how long you want to meditate. Maybe start with 10 minutes (you can use a timer to help).

- You don't need to sit with your legs crossed. A chair is fine, as long as you make sure your spine is well supported. If you use a wheelchair, that can be a great meditation seat.

- If you need to meditate lying down, I'd suggest keeping your eyes open so you're less likely to fall asleep.

- If you like sitting on cushions, make sure your knees are well supported and your back is upright without being tense. Sit high enough to be able to rock gently back and forward on your seat. Try to get comfortable without slumping or arching your back.

- Rest your hands on your lap and relax your shoulders.

- If at any time you feel physically uncomfortable, it's okay to move.

- You don't need to empty your mind of thoughts. Thoughts are natural! When you meditate, your mind will sometimes get quieter on its own.

- Everyone falls asleep sometimes in meditation. Don't sweat it. You might just be tired. Get some rest and try again. Or keep your eyes open.

  Great! Now you're ready to practice.

Learning Kindness

Kindness is something you can learn to develop equally toward all living things and to the earth itself: forests, animals, people, etc. Without kindness, living in harmony with others is impossible.

The Buddha used to say that when you practice kindness, eventually it shines out so strongly from you that it's like the warmth of the sun. Imagine having that effect on people! Imagine how it would be to live with that kind of warmth in your heart.

Of course, a lot of the time we live with the opposite of kindness: people being mean, countries at war, our own reactions to friends or family members when conflicts happen. And sometimes we're not kind to ourselves. Natural feelings come up—disappointment, anxiety, heartbreak, fear—and we get really down on ourselves.

Luckily, we have some very ancient meditations that can help.

Cultivating Kindness

1. All meditation starts with relaxation. Get settled, breathe deeply, and relax your whole body as much as you can.

2. Begin by wishing the best for *yourself,* however else you are feeling. If it helps, you can repeat a simple phrase inside:
    "May I be well, may I be happy, may I find what I need today."
    You can also picture a time in your mind when you felt good. Or try imagining yourself happy in the week ahead. The trick is to let any goodwill in your experience just be there, even if it's faint. No need to push other feelings away: They are real, too. If you get tense in your body, it's okay to stop, breathe, relax, and start over.

3. Imagine a good friend of yours. Now do the same thing toward them: *"May they be well, may they be happy . . ."*

4. This bit's interesting: Imagine someone you see around but don't know well. Try bringing them to mind in the same way, wishing them the best.

5. And here's a challenge: Imagine someone you find difficult or don't like. Maybe in class, or maybe even in your family! Try and set aside your feelings of conflict for a moment or two. See if you can find a way to wish them well, too.

6. To finish, hold in mind yourself and everyone who featured in your meditation today. Sit easy, relax, and enjoy the effects of spending time with a sense of goodwill and kindness.

STORY

The Three Friends

They were inseparable. The Three Friends. That's what they were called. Well, they had names: Ani, Nandi, and Kimbi. But everyone just spoke of "the Three Friends," as if they formed a super-exclusive club. Always together. Keeping themselves to themselves.

On this day, one of them heard that the Stranger was around. Now, the Three Friends knew about the Stranger and were psyched at the thought of meeting someone famed for living a radical life. These days she walked the length of the country just meeting people, talking to them—then moving on. Always leaving a bit of stardust behind.

So, they found her and invited her to where they were hanging out.

The Stranger had heard of the Three Friends, too. She was curious and asked them three questions to see what they were about. First, she asked if they had eaten, and if they were all doing okay.

"Thanks!" Ani said, "We're all good."

Then, the Stranger asked if they actually got along well with each other. Maybe she'd heard they were a clique. Maybe she just wondered why they didn't socialize more.

"Sure, we get on!" Ani replied. "We mix so well it's enough just to be together. Besides, no one else ever comes to see us, though they'd be welcome. We look out for each other. We're like one person, basically."

The Stranger nodded and asked her final question: "How do you manage to get along so well? Don't you get on each other's nerves sometimes?"

Ani thought about that. "Well, it's like this: When I see Nandi and Kimbi need something, I make it my job to provide it, if I can. They see what I need and do the same for me and for each other. Maybe that sounds corny, but really it's not that complicated!"

The Stranger laughed. "I get it!" she said. "That kind of friendship is the whole of life, in the end. Everything else is just details. You three have figured it out. No wonder you're famous: the Three Friends!"

They laughed and talked some more, then she went on her way, smiling into the cool evening.

Think Points

How seriously do you take your friendships? Maybe too seriously sometimes? It can be intense! The path of friendship the Stranger and the Three Friends follow is one of commitment, but it's not clingy. They know how to communicate considerately, with honesty and kindness. They give each other space but also keep each other in mind. A sense of ease and trust flows from there.

People can drift apart or even betray each other's trust. You might behave that way, too, one day. Dealing with the kind of pain that results is tough. But if you make your own commitment, it's like powerful magic against too much sadness. It's also kind of like joy.

I. What do you value most about yourself as a friend?

II. What do you like about your closest friends?

III. What famous person would you choose as a friend? Why?

Square Breathing

Let's explore our experience in the simplest way imaginable: with our breath. If you are breathing, you are alive. If you are alive, you are probably feeling things:

- Confident feelings
- Jealous feelings
- Feeling responsible
- Feeling mad
- Falling in love!
- Falling out of love!
- Proud feelings
- Anxious feelings
- Feelings of excitement

With all these feelings and more, it's amazing we get anything done! And sometimes, even if this is what makes us alive, it's all too much. Then we need to calm ourselves down.

To help with that, here's something you can do anytime, anywhere, without anyone even knowing. Breathing exercises like this are way older than Buddhism. I like to think of the first human beings doing something like it, sitting around a fire, watching the stars overhead.

Drawing the Breath

Like square dancing, square breathing is fun when done standing up outdoors. However, sitting or standing indoors is great, too. Closing your eyes can help you focus and shut out any distractions. But if you're feeling sleepy or self-conscious, you can do it with your eyes open.

1. To start, take a few deep breaths. Get a feel for your body in space: all the air around you, all the space you occupy. Feel your feet on the ground. It's solid. It's holding you up. You can trust gravity.

2. Now we're going to explore breathing in a set pattern that can calm our body and mind. To help, we'll imagine drawing a square, like this:

   i. Breathe in slowly, counting to four: 1-2-3-4. As you draw in your breath, imagine drawing up the left side of a square with your finger.

   ii. Hold your breath for the same count of four. Imagine drawing the top of the square.

   iii. Breathe out for four and—you guessed it—draw down the right side of the square.

   iv. Hold your breath again for four, completing your square at the bottom.

      If at any point you feel a little dizzy, don't worry. You'll likely get used to it, but it's best just to pause until you feel fine.

3. Try the whole square again a few more times. In—Hold—Out—Hold. In—Hold—Out—Hold. Notice how you feel as you do it.

4. When you're done, write down a list of your top 10 feelings—the ones you feel or notice most in your own life. Organize them any way you like: *best to worst, home or school, day or night,* whatever works.

The best way I know of thinking about compassion is this: When someone is sad or having a hard time, to feel compassion is *to shake with them*. That's the original meaning of the Buddhist word that usually gets translated as "compassion": you *tremble with* people.

When we come across someone who is hurting, we can often tell and want to check if they're okay. And when we are hurting, we often want someone to know. Sadly, that doesn't always happen. So, when we are alone with our hurt, it's helpful to be able to develop compassion for ourselves as well as empathy for other people.

Even if we can't just shake it off, we can always *shake with*.

Developing Compassion

1. This meditation builds on developing kindness and goodwill for ourselves. If we can't try and love ourselves, it will be harder to try and love other people. So, however you are feeling, start by relaxing and wishing good things for yourself:

   "May I be well, may I be happy, may I find what I need today."

2. When you're feeling in touch with warmth and wellness, bring to mind a friend who is having a hard time. Remember, compassion is when your sense of kindness and goodwill meets with—*shakes with*—someone's unhappiness. You can't take their pain away, but you can wish them well with your whole being, shining on them like a small sun.

   Take it gently with this. It's strong! There's a knack to it: Breathe easy, and try to stay nice and relaxed as you sit. Let your heart respond.

3. You can't do this wrong. Notice what's going on for you. Maybe you feel sad in response. Maybe you get a bit tense thinking about your friend's difficulties, and your mind wanders. Whatever happens is fine. Just breathe, smile warmly at yourself in your mind, and turn back to your friend. Keep encouraging your sense of kindness and encouragement to flow naturally toward them.

4. At any time, be free to expand this sense of connection in your imagination, as widely as you like. Turn the warmth toward anyone who is struggling or suffering (even people you find difficult). Let yourself feel what you feel and respond with kindness and encouragement.

Then, when you're ready, gently draw your meditation to a close, breathing easy . . .

STORY

My Enemy, My Teacher

"OMG! He's taking *who*? *That* guy? You have got to be kidding me."

The students were huddled together, whispering. The sky was blue, the air fresh and bright. Yet here they were, hanging around the yard like a small thundercloud, buzzing angrily, getting ready to rain.

"We should totally complain. We'll say we're not going if *he's* going. He's so *annoying*!"

They were Atisha's students. Atisha, who'd just been asked to go and teach Buddhism in another country. Atisha, who was taking them, his beloved students, along for the adventure. He was the rock star! They were his entourage! So why was he bringing that super irritating, not-even-funny, local kid?

Of course, Atisha didn't think of himself as a celebrity. And he certainly wasn't taking them to bask in his glory. But they hadn't gotten that yet. So they chattered away for a while longer, getting deep into all the drama, then decided to go and see him.

Atisha listened. Then he was silent. By the time he spoke, they were fidgeting like chickens pecking at the ground. Only, in the silence, they were pecking at their own minds.

Atisha knew the kid they objected to. He lived nearby and worked around the school on weekends. It was true: He could be very irritating. Always making mean jokes. Always arguing about obvious things. Always looking for attention. It was painful to watch. And that had really struck him: Even he—"famous" Atisha, who everybody had such faith in—had moments when he wanted the boy to just stop, just to shut up. Ah . . .

That's when he'd thought of it: *I should invite this kid to come. I will teach him, and he, I think, will teach me something, too.*

Now he spoke to the nervous students. His voice was rich and low, but not angry. His words were heartfelt, which surprised them all.

"Haven't you heard anything I've been telling you? We can't pick and choose who we are kind to. I don't want to be surrounded by people who are only along for the ride. I want to learn patience, and I want to be with friends who can learn it, too! Without patience, we might as well give up. It's the best tool we have for making things right in this world. I've a feeling this boy could be the making of our journey."

And so he was. But that's another story.

Think Points

We can find important lessons in the unlikeliest of ways and places. When you start being curious about your own reactions to things, you can learn a lot about how you might change! It's all good data about you.

I. How might you learn patience and kindness from someone you find difficult?

II. When you think of people you don't like, do you think they want the same things you do?

III. How do you feel when you see people disagreeing online or around the dinner table?

ACTIVITY

Ethical People Watching

This is another outdoor activity to try, but it's fine if you need to be indoors instead. The main thing is to be able to see lots of people. Don't worry, no public interaction is required. Look out the window onto a busy street. Or hang out at the mall, sitting on a bench. I guess you could even do this exercise online, watching a live video feed of a busy Tokyo or New York City street!

We're going to do some ethical people watching. First, some ground rules:

- Let's not stare at anyone or make them uncomfortable

- Definitely no photographing

- No shouting out to anyone

- Being around crowds can be intense for some. If you feel over-whelmed, just close your eyes and breathe the way we did in the square breathing exercise (page 11). Then, take a break.

Ready? Time to be curious about the ways you take in other people.

1. Sit a distance from the folks you're observing. As they pass, just notice them. If it's crowded, you can let your eyes drift easily from face to face. If individuals walk by, imagine them like clouds floating past you in a blue sky. Just notice them, taking in their faces as they go.

2. Notice their different ages: young kids, old people, babies, people the same age as your parents, other teens. Notice how you feel about faces of different ages.

3. Now, notice any thoughts you have about people who pass by. No need to give yourself a hard time for being judgmental—it's natural. But try to notice, and check in with how you are feeling if you get caught up in a story about anyone you see.

4. Think about where individuals might be coming from, where they are going. Imagine their lives: *going home for dinner*, *walking the dog*, *meeting friends*.

5. Finally, take a few minutes and try silently wishing everyone well, coming and going. Just as before in the meditation: *"May they be well, may they be happy, may they find what they need today."*

At home, try writing down or recording your impressions of the people you saw. You can start to get a sense of any patterns in the way your mind works emotionally around other people. Look for the same kinds of patterns coming up throughout the day at home and in school. Check your notes a week or two later and see if it brings up any new insights for you.

Sharing the Joy

In this meditation, we're going to build outward as we did before, from ourselves to others. This time, our emotional attention won't be meeting suffering; it will be meeting joy.

Most of us know what happiness feels like. But what is joy? Is there a difference? Well, like suffering, joy can be a tricky idea to get your head around. So, rather than talk any more about it, let's see if we can get a feel for it instead.

Meditating on Joy

1. Try to relax your body. Start by wishing for good things in your own life. However you're doing today, tell yourself, *"May I be well, may I be happy, may I find what I need."* This can be your secret superpower. You can always come back to it, anytime.

2. Bring to mind someone you know who is usually positive and cheerful. It can be one of your friends or someone you really look up to. Whoever you choose, it's not that they're never sad; they just deal with stuff well and are good to be around.

   - How does it feel when you think of them?

   - Imagine them experiencing real, deep happiness and contentment in their life.

   - Let your appreciation flow toward them in your mind.

3. Now, bring to mind someone you see around but don't really know. See if you can imagine them the same way: well and happy, feeling fulfilled in their life.

4. As you meditate like this, notice what's going on for you: in your body, in your mind, in your heart. Don't worry if you find this harder than you expected. Maybe you just feel sad or anxious today. Your meditation still counts! Keep in touch with a sense of wanting kindness for yourself, however you feel right now.

   Make sure you are breathing nice and easy. If any tension has crept back into your body, it's always good to relax your shoulders, face, and hands.

5. Try expanding any sense you have of positivity, happiness, and joy: to friends, family, and even people you don't like.

   Imagine happiness bubbling up around the world: babies being born, families together, friends hanging out, lovers meeting, people feeling good and doing what they find fulfilling.

   Let yourself feel your responses, whatever they are. Spend a few more minutes connecting with joy in the world.

6. When you're ready, bring your meditation to a close and let go of any effort you've been making. Rest easy wherever you are, and allow the effects of this meditation to soak in.

STORY

Eight or Eighty?

Once there was a queen who, like that young prince we met earlier, had everything she could ever want: all the money, all the jewels, all the *everyone* doing whatever she ordered. But this queen was bored. She had lost interest in all her usual pastimes, the news, what was going on with her friends. Boredom wasn't supposed to happen. Not to her.

At breakfast, someone mentioned that a famous Buddhist wanderer had just arrived in the city. The queen became excited at the idea of maybe hearing some new ideas from this teacher. Buddhism was supposed to be super cool. She'd heard of meditation. She'd heard of Buddhists living happily in mountain caves eating only nettles. She'd even heard of nuns and monks who were amazing at kung fu! She had to meet this person, who would surely reveal what to do to get rid of boredom.

Later that day, the wanderer stood in the great hall of the palace. The painted ceilings were so high that they looked like a window into another world, a magical realm. Everything was gold or silver or made of smooth, precious stone. The wanderer thought it was beautiful. "One day," she figured, "the foxes will make their home here, and weeds will sprout out of every corner."

Just as she was daydreaming about trees growing up around the marble pillars, a guard came and summoned her before the queen. It was a long walk! Endless corridors. But finally she reached the many steps that led up to the queen's throne. She stopped there and bowed.

The queen didn't invite her up. Instead, she called down:

"Greetings, traveler. I wish to ask you some questions about Buddhism."

"Of course, Your Majesty."

"What is the ultimate meaning of life?"

The wanderer raised her eyes.

"Life is *vast*. It's certainly not about being powerful—or holy."

The queen frowned and said, "I thought you were a Buddhist! Who is this facing me?"

The teacher shrugged: "I don't know."

The queen was flabbergasted! Then she asked:

"Well, tell me this at least: What is the secret of Buddhist wisdom?"

The wanderer thought for a second, then answered clear as a bell:

"Cease to do evil, learn to do good, purify your heart."

The queen was shocked. "Is that it? Even a child of eight can understand *that*!"

The wanderer bowed again and replied: "Yes, but even a person of eighty cannot put it into practice."

Think Points

It's not enough just to learn about ideas—in Buddhism or anything else. To really understand something, you need to get ahold of the emotional spirit of the ideas, too. That's what meditation is for: to let ideas go deep and maybe change your life for the better. When it works, it's kind of like magic.

I. What do you usually do when you're bored? Does it help?

II. Why might the wanderer say she doesn't know who she is?

III. If you could ask one question to someone you thought knew everything, what would you ask?

ACTIVITY

Multiplayer Positivity

In my Buddhist team at work, we sometimes do this thing together we call "Rejoicing in Merits." It's basically just a fancy name for spending time together and saying what it is we like, admire, appreciate, and even love about each other.

Now, that may sound weird to you. Or it may sound awesome. Or scary! I know I can still feel pretty awkward about doing it: I don't usually like being the center of attention or having people be very direct with me about emotions. But the thing is, this activity has really helped me over the years. It teaches me a lot about how to love myself, and how to be positive with other people.

Here's a different take on it. After a few rounds, I guarantee you'll have heard a lot of good things about yourself. And who couldn't use that sometimes?

1. Gather three or more friends or family members. This works best with four or more people, but I'm sure you can improvise even if there's two or 10 of you!

   Some people prefer sitting in a room where everyone can have more personal space. Others are happy to sit around a table together.

2. Give a large piece of paper to each person. Have them write their name and fold the paper in two, with their name on the outside.

   When that's done, everyone passes their paper to the person to their left.

3. Have everyone write down something they like, admire, or love about the person named on the piece of paper they're holding. When everyone has done this, they should refold the paper and pass it on to the next person.

4. At the end, everyone's paper comes back to them, and they read it quietly to themselves. Then, if all are comfortable with it, mix up the papers and get everyone to read someone else's praises out loud.

5. You can go around twice or even three times if you're feeling inspired!

P.S.: You can also do this via a message thread. Assign a private thread for each person to someone different in the group. For example, to send something positive about Sean, message Shanice; to send something you like about Shanice, message Suki.

Here's another skill to add to your collection. It's a meditation that acknowledges the mixture of both happiness and sadness we often experience. It can help us go deeper into a sense of respect for everyone, including ourselves. In the end, we're all in this together.

Equalizing Positivity

1. As usual, we'll start by making sure we're in touch with trying to build some kindness toward ourselves. It's the strongest foundation for this or any other meditation:

    "May I be well, may I be happy, may I give myself what I need today."

2. When you're in touch with this kindness, turn to someone in your mind who you don't really know. As before, someone who's kind of neutral in your life: not a friend; not someone you have strong feelings for either way.

    See if you can turn the same warmth toward them. Take a moment to think about their life: Like you, they are happy sometimes, feel bright and ready for the day ahead. Like you, they struggle sometimes: They can be upset, feel depressed, or can't handle school or other people.

3. Now, consider the idea that both these things—having a hard time, having a good time—don't last forever. Something always changes. This person you have in mind has a life ahead of them full of the joy and sadness of being human, just like you.

    Notice what feelings arise. Try not to get caught up in them or push them away. Just let them be there, as if a small rabbit crept close to you and you're being careful not to scare it off.

    It's okay to take little breaks: relax in your body, breathe deeply, and come back to your reflections.

4. Now, do the same thing thinking of a good friend. Do this for a few minutes. Next, do the same thing thinking of someone you find difficult.

5. Gather together in your mind everyone so far: yourself, the person you don't really know, your friend, and the person you find difficult.

    Reflect one last time on the fact that all of you are sad sometimes and happy sometimes, and that all of you really want to be well.

    Try and turn your sense of warmth equally toward everyone. Let yourself feel what you feel. When you're ready, let your meditation come to an end.

Kindness Is Wisdom

Remember the prince who fled from the palace? We left him as he went off to search for the meaning of life. Well, this is years later. And guess what? He hasn't gotten anywhere.

Maybe that's unfair. He learned a lot about his emotions and how to work with them. But the truth of existence? Not so much.

So, there he was, standing at the edge of a river. And he was learning now about the limits of his body. You see, he'd been doing some dumb stuff. Someone told him if he fasted—stopped eating much—his senses would sharpen and he'd understand everything. His senses sharpened a little bit, for a day or so. And he certainly learned to handle some new pain. But he'd also learned that this was not worth anything on its own. After weeks of tiny amounts of food, he was exhausted and very weak.

He thought back to that first day after he had escaped the palace. He had been exhilarated then! Now, he felt as if he had run out of road.

Not knowing what to do, he sat under a nearby tree and tried to meditate, but he was too tired. So he dozed, wondering how he might find something to eat in the middle of nowhere.

Soon, a young woman came along the river path. When she wasn't at school, she took charge of a herd of fine goats, keeping alive a local tradition of shepherding that ran in her family. She milked the goats regularly, and otherwise let them roam free.

The young woman, Sujata, saw the thin, ill-looking stranger slumped against the tree trunk and stopped.

"Hey, mister. Are you okay?"

The prince half opened his eyes and looked up, trying to smile. Sujata was alarmed.

"Whoa! You are sick!"

She knelt down beside him and asked if she could check his temperature. He said yes, so she placed one cool hand on his forehead and looked for signs of any other trouble.

"When did you last eat?"

He could only nod weakly, confirming her suspicions that he was dehydrated and hungry.

"Here," she offered, helping him drink from a water bottle she had with her. "It's goat's milk. It'll help you get your strength back."

"Thank you," he croaked, reviving already. Then, she gave him a little sweet rice left over from the lunch she'd packed. It seemed as if he would be okay.

"You good? Get some rest. And whenever you like, come to the village. Look for the sign of the goat on my door! I'm Sujata, by the way."

He took her hand and thanked her. As he watched her walk off down the path, it was as if his mind cleared after a long, long fog. He smiled, then settled down with his back against the strong trunk of the tree.

Think Points

Even when we do what we think is best, our choices don't always make us happy.

I. Has anyone ever shown you kindness when you really didn't expect it?

II. Who is the wisest person you know, and why?

Your Relationship Mandala

Have you ever heard of a *mandala*? They're kind of like maps, but ones that work in multiple dimensions and take you to a mythic place. They remind me of the "teleport maps" you sometimes find in video games: they give an overview of where you are and can help you move around in unexpected ways.

Mandalas can also just be patterns—sometimes simple, sometimes complicated. But they're always beautiful and full of meaning.

So, mandalas can be useful for mapping the patterns of our own thoughts or emotional connections. Let's make a mandala of your relationships with other people.

You can do this with just paper and a pen or pencil (use different colors if you like). You can also do it on a tablet, phone, or computer. Capture it the way that works best for you.

1. Like any world, yours needs continents. These can be actual places or groups of people in your life. Let's start with four main areas, which you can draw out as you like—any shape, any size, any color. Each will represent one of the following:

   - **Home and family** (This might be more than one continent if you have two families. Pets allowed!)

   - **School** (teachers, friends, and acquaintances)

   - **Friends** (There's bound to be overlap here; also includes romantic interests.)

   - **Heroes** (sports, arts, literature, fictional, or real)

Notice if you drew any of these in a different size or if they are all the same. If you want, resize them according to what seems most important to you.

2. Okay! Now mark your own position in the mandala however you want. Where will you represent yourself? At the edges? In the center? Somewhere else?

3. Now, add anyone you know to any of your "continents." Write their names, along with three things about them you like, admire, appreciate, or love.

4. Make arrows or pathways (like this: --------) between people and/or the different qualities in your mandala. Maybe your teacher is friends with your aunt. Maybe you look up to your dad and your favorite athlete because they're both so dedicated.

5. Look at your mandala. Can you see any patterns emerging? Would you like to add any more continents? For example, you could have one for a club, a workplace, or a single class in school.

You can redo this, trying different shapes, categories, and arrangements. You now have a first map of all your relationships—and some of your favorite qualities of your family and friends. It's helpful—and can feel good—to stand back sometimes and look at all your connections. Try bringing this out and looking at it the next time you're feeling alone.

MEDITATION

Being in the Blue Sky

So far, we've tried out meditations that can help us:

- Cultivate kindness and goodwill toward ourselves and others

- Develop compassion when we and anyone else we encounter is having a bad time

- Explore how we can share in other people's joy and good fortune

- Respond positively, knowing everyone has happiness and sadness in common

Here's a meditation that draws together all you've explored so far. First, some preparation:

- It's another outside meditation, standing and walking if you're able.

- If you're in a wheelchair, try this somewhere you can move around without others being in your path.

- If you're on your feet, try being on some grass, if you can.

- If you can't get outside, you can also do this at home, sitting or moving as you're able.

Gathering

1. First, stand or sit still. Keep your eyes open for now. Really take in your surroundings: the sights, sounds, smells, and the feeling of air on your skin. As you relax your body, feel your weight on the earth. It's supporting you. Now, look at the sky. Take in the great space above you stretching to the horizon.

2. When you're ready, start to walk or wheel. Pay attention to your breath as you move. Feel your feet or wheels on the ground. If you aren't able to move through space right now, try mimicking movements by tapping out a rhythm with your hands on your thighs.

   Let your movements be your guide. Move wherever or however you want to. Let yourself be grounded by your breathing, your steady motion. You can count your steps or arm movements if it helps you focus.

3. After a few minutes, stop somewhere you feel good about and be still. If you like, close your eyes. Picture in your mind—imagine, or feel a sense of—a great blue sky overhead and all around you. It's a beautiful, safe space. What shade of blue is it? Are there clouds or is it clear? Are you standing or floating?

4. In your mind, invite into this space anyone you like: family, friends, classmates, heroes, enemies, loves, teachers.

   Enjoy their "presence" with you. Wish everyone well, including yourself, in whatever way seems to work, with or without words.

   "May we be well. May we be happy. May we live without fear, and with confidence. May we find what we need in the world."

   When you're ready, finish the meditation with a little bow to everyone in your imagination.

CHAPTER 2

Being in Your Body

We shake when we're frightened or anxious. We get warmer when we're embarrassed or see someone we like. Our mind responds emotionally to our senses: *That's soft, I like it! That tastes too hot, I don't like it!*

In this chapter, we'll be exploring our experience *in the body*, and how Buddhism encourages positive body relationships.

You've heard a lot about the big physical changes that happen in your teenage years—perhaps you're already experiencing some. Actually, similar changes continue throughout life (from becoming an adult, to being middle-aged, to being an elderly person!). Mindfulness of your body, breathing, and the ways you hold yourself and move can help you feel more alive as you grow and change, whatever age you are.

Sometimes, in order to know what's going on, we have to be still. Other times, we need to wheel, walk, run, dance, swim, or jump. Let's get going . . .

The Sea Turtle

Song was a farm kid, proud to help her parents sow and harvest onions every year. She loved the way the earth felt under her fingers; she loved how fresh green onion stalks felt in her hands as she pulled them gently out of the ground.

But Song felt like an uprooted onion herself sometimes. She was restless. She wanted to see exotic places, meet wonderful strangers, taste what life had to offer.

Song's neighbor was an old man called Popa. Her family would do small kindnesses for him most days: picking up groceries, collecting his mail. He always had enough onions!

One day, Song knocked on his door. Popa was writing at the kitchen table. He had been a doctor and still loved to study and learn new things. He was glad to see her, and as they talked, Song confided that she hoped to leave the farm one day. She was worried her parents would be heartbroken.

Popa thought for a while. "When I was around your age, I couldn't get away from home fast enough," he recalled. "I wanted to see the world. Eventually, I did!

"I don't know what's best for your life, Song. Maybe you should root yourself here. Maybe you should sprout elsewhere. Either way, it's good to appreciate what you do have: a healthy body, a loving home, the earth beneath your feet."

Then, Popa told her an old Buddhist story:

"There was once a sea turtle so majestic that it only came to the surface of the ocean once every hundred years to breathe. Perhaps it was related to the turtle that, in ancient times, was said to hold up the world.

"Now, on the surface of the ocean floated a piece of wood with a hole in it only slightly larger than the turtle's head. And one day, of all the impossible things, the turtle rose to take its hundred-year breath— and pop! Its head went right through the hole in the wood, which it now wore like a life vest!"

Popa chuckled away at this, but seeing Song's doubtful face, he said more seriously:

"Song, the sheer coincidence of the turtle's head going through a hole in a single piece of driftwood floating on the sea: That's *more likely* than human beings evolving over billions of years in this truly vast universe! So, that makes it more likely than you having a body that could soon carry you away from here—and, who knows, maybe one day bring you back again.

"It will not always feel like it, but your human life is a gift more precious than anything. May you always make your peace with it, wherever you go."

Song nodded, catching something important in her friend's words. Now she knew how she wanted to live.

Think Points

Our bodies, hearts, and minds don't always feel precious. Sometimes they bring pain or sadness. It's normal to feel unsure about it all, and it's okay to ask for help with living.

I. What do you value most about your body? Why?

II. How old would you like to live to? Why?

III. Who do you go to for advice?

Lying Up the Wall

Building on the last chapter, this practice can give you a better sense in your body of what is going on emotionally, because it shakes up your normal way of experiencing things and lets some fresh perspective come in. Literally, you'll be turning the world upside down for a few minutes—and seeing how you feel. It's kind of weird and fun!

1. Sit on your bed or the floor, cross-legged or with your knees up, facing the wall. Have your feet touching the wall if you can (it's okay if you can't!).

2. Now, lie back and scooch your bottom as close to the wall as you can get it. This part's awkward, so do whatever feels easy. Make sure your head is supported with a cushion or pillow if you need it. If this isn't a position your body can take, try sitting and tilting your head back—or just lie flat.

3. Your legs will have nowhere to go but up! Have them any way you like: bent in a comfortable position with the soles of your feet resting flat on the wall, or as straight as you can with your heels resting in a gentle stretch.

    Congratulations! You are now lying up the wall.

4. If you have room on either side, stretch your arms wide. Then, try folding your hands on your chest as if you're sleeping like a great queen or king.

5. Take a few intentional breaths in whatever position most suits your mood. Try this:

    - Take three deep, slow breaths. Focus on each phase of each breath as it comes and goes, like watching waves break as the tide rolls in and out.

    - Now, just breathe normally and notice how you're feeling.

    - What's this like with your eyes open or closed?

- Are you holding any tension in your body? Where?

- Try the three breaths again. Feel free to find your own comfortable body position and breathing (for example, try hugging your knees or changing the number of breaths).

6. Let your mind float for a minute or two. Look around the room— all the strange angles, unfamiliar corners. See if you can relax into being upside down.

7. If you are comfortable, stay there as long as you like.

What I love about this practice is that I can do it whenever I'm alone in a safe space. But I've also done this with friends, sometimes talking for hours!

P.S.: It's okay if you fall asleep!

MEDITATION

Checking in with Your Body

Before any meditation, it's always a good idea to check in with your body. After all, you're not meditating as a giant disembodied brain! Though, when our eyes are closed, it can sometimes feel like that—we can get so caught up in our heads we forget we even have a body.

Other times, we can't focus on anything *except* our body: Maybe we're carrying some discomfort; maybe we're feeling really self-conscious. Either way, we need to balance our awareness. This is where mindfulness of our body can help.

A Mindful Body Scan

Take a minute to make sure you're really comfortable. If you need a refresher, go back and check out "Getting Ready to Meditate" (page 5).

1. Just as meditating on your emotions starts with the body, meditating on your body begins with wanting the best for yourself. So, find your own way to wish yourself well. Here's a suggestion:

    "May I be well and at ease. May my body be comfortable and my mind be at peace."

2. You're going to scan through your body from top to toe, relaxing as much as possible as you go. Get as detailed, or stay as broad, as you like. You're just looking to relax deeply—nothing more!

    Start by breathing easy. You're going to try imagining breathing into each area as you focus your attention there. Let's start with the crown of your head. Can you feel where that is?

    Now, work your way down either side of your body, or both sides, pausing for a few moments whenever it feels right to take in different parts:

    - Scalp, hair, ears

    - Eyebrows, eyelids, eyeballs

    - The bridge of your nose, nostrils

    - Upper and lower lips, your tongue and teeth

    - Cheekbones, jaw, chin . . .

3. Now, do the same thing for the rest of your body in stages, breathing into your:

    - Neck and shoulders (really let those shoulders go!)

    - Arms and hands

    - Chest and belly

- Back, upper and lower (try and feel each vertebra in your spine)

- Private parts and your bottom (don't leave them out!)

- Thighs, front and back

- Knees, both sides

- Calves and shins

- Ankles and heels

- Feet, right to the tips of your toes

4. You've traveled a long way in your mind—your body is a whole country! Feel free to take your attention all the way back up.

5. When you finish, sit still for a minute longer with your eyes open. How do you feel now?

STORY

An Arrow in the Eye

Since he was eight, Mal had been trying to learn facts about *everything*. He'd read every book he could find with titles like *Ask Me Why!* and *Secrets of the Universe.* He borrowed old encyclopedias from the library. Wikipedia was his favorite website. "One day," he thought, "I'm going to have all the answers!"

By the time he was 14, Mal was stuffed full of facts. If there was a quiz or trivia game to be played, you'd want him on your side. He ignored all the other things he might do: learning to cook or code, exercise and sports, hanging out with kids from his class. Instead, Mal spent more and more time at his computer, looking stuff up.

One day, a new teacher appeared in school. She was a replacement for Ms. Cullen, who was off for six weeks having a baby. Mal had enjoyed Ms. Cullen's philosophy class, though he liked his facts better.

Ms. Sabasava arrived. On her first day, she got them to walk around outside, slowly and carefully, *for 10 whole minutes*. She asked them to think about their bodies, feel their feet on the ground, follow their breath in and out. Back in the classroom, she had them sit and do Buddhist meditation instead of talking. It drove Mal crazy. He wasn't learning *anything*!

After a few weeks, Mal cracked. He stayed behind after class. Ms. Sabasava didn't seem surprised.

"Hi! Mal, isn't it? How can I help you?"

"Why are you making us do all this? It's not teaching us anything!"

Ms. Sabasava looked at him curiously. "Okay, what would you like to know?"

Mal was flummoxed. "Uh . . . well, the answers to questions, like: *How did we get here? Is space never-ending? What happens after we die?*"

She smiled at him, and now he felt uncertain. "Imagine someone fired a poison arrow at you, Mal, and it hit you right in the eye. What would you want to do?"

Mal was shocked. "Whoa! Pull it out, I guess. Then go to the emergency room!"

"Exactly! Would you say, 'Before I pull out this arrow, I want to know what it's made of. What color it is. The name of the person who assembled it at the factory, and their parents' names. I want to know how well it flies, what the poison is made of'?"

"Of course not! I'd bleed to death." Mal protested.

"Well then," Ms. Sabasava finished, as the bell rang for next class, "perhaps you need a different kind of learning, Mal—if you want to be happy. Having answers isn't everything."

She smiled again and left him standing there. It was a mic drop. Mal felt his mind opening up like a starfish.

Think Points

Facts aren't the same thing as knowledge. And knowledge isn't the same thing as understanding. If you wait around to try and know everything, life might pass you by.

I. What do you think it is impossible to know?

II. How might paying attention to your body and breath help you learn better?

III. Are there questions without answers that really bug you?

ACTIVITY

Getting Out of the Story

One of the smartest observations the Buddha made was that when things cause us sadness or pain, it's not just because something bad happened—it's also because we get caught up in a million conflicted thoughts and feelings about it.

You know: someone says something to you—maybe a small remark—and suddenly, "She said that because she thinks *this* about me!" Or "He's *never* trusted me—and now this latest insult!" And on and on . . .

Now, the person *may* have been insensitive or mean, or they may not have meant any of that other stuff. The Buddha's point is: In our upset, we're adding a big story or drama *around* what actually happened. And that can hurt us, too.

This exercise, rooted in your body, can help you learn to walk some of that back.

1. Take a moment to make sure you're comfortable. Breathe easy.
   If you like, you can do a quick, relaxing body scan.
   As in a meditation, wish yourself well.

2. Think about something that's upsetting you. It's okay to still feel upset, so take your time.
   Notice if any story is building up in your mind around what happened—maybe there are lots of thoughts or emotions swirling around that keep you feeling defensive.
   Now, try to gently strip it back to the bare facts of what happened. For example:

   • *Not:* They said *that*, and that meant *this*, and I know because *that other thing* . . .

   • *More like*: They said that thing . . .

   Just the description, nothing else.

3. Spend a few minutes with your experience. Can you stay with the bare facts? Does the story return?
   This is hard, so give yourself a break! Try relaxing your body again. You might even smile if you catch your mind running away with its story.

4. Can you set aside the story for a few moments? Imagine pressing pause on the audio or putting the storybook back on the shelf.
   Now, let's get in touch with how you're feeling. For example, if you're lonely or hurt, where is the feeling in your body? See if you can breathe into wherever this feeling sits.

5. Put your hand on your heart. Take a few deep breaths and wish yourself well. If you're upset with another person, try wishing them well, too.

     When you're done, write down or capture anything you noticed.

This is a great strategy to try anytime. Everyone's mind gets carried away, and anyone can learn to get out of the story.

Deeper into the Breath

Throughout this book, we've explored:

- Moving while being aware of our breath

- Different ways our breath can help us relax

- Breathing as a way to work through anxiety and stress

This breath meditation is pretty ancient—in fact, it's quite like the first one the Buddha learned!

Following Our Breath

Our breath is something we always carry with us, whether we're sitting, moving, or lying down. So, you can do this anywhere, making it your own as you need.

1. Take some time to settle. Try a few deeper breaths, shaking out any tension you notice.

     How are you feeling? Good or not, gently try and find a way to wish the best for yourself today.

2. We'll start following along with our breathing. To help with focus, mark the start of each breath with a simple, silent count in your mind. Like this:

- Count 1, breathe in, breathe out. Count 2, breathe in, breathe out.

- Keep going, breathing and counting from 1 through 10.

Everyone gets distracted and loses count sometimes. I've learned to smile when I notice. Just start again at 1 and have fun with it!

3. Next, a small change. See if you can feel the difference when you count at the *end* of each breath:

- Breathe in, breathe out, count 1. Breathe in, breathe out, count 2.

- Again, from 1 through 10.

4. Are you still relaxed? Notice how you're feeling. Now it's time to go deeper. Follow your breath as before, only now, *drop the counting*:

- Try to trace the flow of air as it comes in, passes through your body, and leaves again. Be curious, see if you can stay with it. Air into breath, breath back into air . . .

- Imagine it nourishing all the parts of you, bringing rich oxygen and life.

- If your mind wanders off, gently come back to your body and breath.

5. Ready to go deeper still?

- See if you can rest your attention wherever you first feel the sensation of your in-breath. It's maybe around your nostrils, lips, or throat. Maybe in your chest or belly.

- Noticing is like watching a hummingbird or dragonfly land on a flower. See if you can stay with that delicate place of contact between the air and your body.

- It's a tiny moment, but imagine one breath is an ocean or universe you can immerse yourself in!

6. Draw your meditation to an end. Just sit and rest, enjoying the space . . .

STORY

Under the Rose Apple

Let's check back with our prince. How's it going on his quest to find the truth about life?

Well, it's a beautiful, cool evening by the river. A forest stirs with birdsong as the sun melts pink into the horizon.

Someone is sitting under a tree. He *used to be* a prince, but who is he now?

Inside he felt nameless, unknown, unloved. He'd been wandering for years and ended up here. In the middle of nowhere. There was no one now. Sujata, who'd saved his life with her kindness, was long gone, back to the village. Maybe he should take her up on that offer of care and friendship with her family.

He looked up and smiled in recognition. This was a rose apple tree! The red fruit and greenest leaves, as in a fairy tale: red like Snow

White's apple, green like the heart of life. Something about the colors made him remember . . .

That's right, he'd been a boy, around 10 or 11. Sitting under another tree just like this one, watching his father, the king, take part in a ceremony out in the fields. The farmers were digging up the earth to mark the beginning of spring. It was time to plant rice and seeds and let life take over.

He smiled to himself. Another memory bubbled up. He'd felt so happy and at peace that day. He'd closed his eyes and sat still in the dappled light under the leaves, only aware of his breath as it rose and fell. Maybe it was only minutes, but it seemed like days. He'd gotten so deeply absorbed, as if time itself went away.

Just as it had back then, the trunk of this tree felt strong and good against his back. The bark felt like his own skin. If he could have merged into it, become part of the tree right there and then, he would have.

"I've spent all this time walking and walking. But in the end, I found nothing," he thought, a little sadly. Then he checked himself.

"No, *not* nothing. I reached this place, this time. And I found my childhood here. Maybe there isn't anything magic to be discovered. At least not somewhere else. All the magic I need is right here, right now. It *must* be. I wonder . . ."

He settled back. The tree was supporting him. It felt as if the birds were supporting him. The sweet evening air filled his lungs. His chest rose and fell. His eyes closed like a boy dreaming again, only he wasn't asleep. And in his mind, he went back to the beginning with everything, to the source of all life: He began to pay attention to his breath. And the river flowed on beside him . . .

Think Points

I. When have you felt happiest and most at peace in your body?

II. When you think about things, would you say you live more in the past, present, or future?

III. The prince feels like a nobody. Do you know what that feels like? What do you think would help?

Be in the Place Where You Are

If you're able to get outside, this exercise is best done in the open. It also works well indoors. And it's just as good sitting down or standing up.

1. If you know your compass points, start by facing north. You could look it up or ask someone which way is north.

Alternatively, set your starting direction as 12 o'clock in your mind, then make a quarter turn each stage.

2. Let's ground and center ourselves. Stand or sit with your hands by your side (or resting in your lap). Eyes open or closed. Your shoulders relaxing. Feel the earth supporting you.

Start with a couple of deeper breaths to help you arrive, then breathe easy.

3. Open your eyes and notice five things you can see within your field of vision (it's okay to turn your head). What stands out for you? Is it color? Shape? Appearance? Is it an object, a building, an animal, a person?

If you're not sighted, you can start with whatever sense is sharpest for you. Or just be present with your body for a few minutes, enjoying the space.

4. Now, turn to face east (a quarter turn to the right). Notice four things you hear. Do you like some sounds more than others? Are any birds singing?

   If you can't hear well, choose a different sense. Or just savor the moments till you're ready for another stage.

   You can close or open your eyes at any time now.

5. Turn to the south (another quarter turn). Notice three things you can touch or feel with your body. For example, the grass, a breeze on your face, spokes on your wheelchair. It's okay to bend and touch something.

6. Turn to the west (a quarter turn). Notice two things you smell. This might be stronger indoors, or maybe you catch the smell of fresh-cut grass, wood smoke, or city garbage smells in the air!

7. Finally, turn back to the north (the last quarter turn). Notice anything you can taste: salty, sweet, sour, umami.

8. When you're ready, you can end or start over if you like.

This exercise might help anytime you're feeling anxious, because it puts you in touch with your body and breath and widens your mind's focus.

If you are indoors, try it in different rooms: bathroom, basement, kitchen. Or, try it in different landscapes: the football field, your yard after dark, up a mountain, by the ocean, at a park, or in a cemetery (with friends!).

As we saw in chapter 1, just moving or walking mindfully is a calming practice that can help us stay grounded and in touch with our body.

You can try this meditation in different ways:

- As described, wheeling or walking outside.

- In a room where you have enough space to move back and forward a decent distance.

- Sitting still. Think about a place you know and imagine walking or moving through it in your mind. Tap out your imagined movements with your hands.

Movement Meditation

1. Wherever you are, start by being still. Let your eyes close. Take a few deeper breaths to help you relax and be present.

   As you sit or stand, imagine being strong like a tree, your roots deep in the earth. Feel your weight supported by the ground or floor, or by your wheelchair. Enjoy the experience of just being supported.

2. Take in any sounds, smells, or tastes you may be aware of. Feel the air on your skin, especially if you're outside. Is it warm or cool? Notice the light through your eyelids, its color and glow.

3. When you feel settled, open your eyes. Now, keeping your gaze on the ground or floor just ahead of you, start to move carefully in whatever direction seems good, keeping clear of other people.

   Breathe normally. To help you stay aware of your movements, walk or push yourself as carefully as you can.

Go as slow or as fast as you like, but try to pay close attention to how your arms or legs move. If you're walking, try to feel each part of your foot as it lands. You can be deliberate about it: the heel, then the flat of your foot, then the toes.

If you're wheeling manually, try to be extra aware of each rotation of your chair, each phase of your arm movement as you push, and your forward momentum.

4. Stop every so often and close your eyes again. Shake out any tension in your hands and shoulders.

   Breathe easy. Check that you're still taking in all that richness from your senses: light, touch, taste, smell, sound.

5. Open your eyes and continue moving. Notice if stopping and starting changes anything. Maybe you can sense the air on your face more clearly each time you move; maybe your breathing is different.

6. When you want to finish, stop one last time. Close your eyes and take in everything that's going on, then bring your meditation to an end.

STORY

Necklace of Fingers

Okay, here's a story you have to hear. It's about a bandit called Angulimala. What does his name mean? *Necklace of fingers*. Seriously!

Of course, those fingers used to belong to people. Unlucky travelers who'd run into him in the woods.

Angulimala had collected 99 fingers, and now nobody traveled alone at night. So, he hung out closer to the village, even in daytime. He was obsessed with that hundredth finger—then his necklace would be complete . . .

The Buddha happened to pass through and heard about it from the villagers.

"Where does this guy live?"

"In the woods! He haunts the paths like a murderous ghost."

"Point the way," the Buddha requested thoughtfully. "I'd like to pay him a visit."

They begged their guest not to go.

The forest was dark, a thick canopy of green so dense that the sunlight hardly crept in. But the Buddha set off down the path as if out for a morning stroll. Hidden behind a tree, Angulimala was watching, excited to finish his gross necklace.

He began to stalk the Buddha, gradually faster and faster, ready to pounce like a tiger . . . only something weird was happening. The faster Angulimala moved, the *further away* his victim got! And when he slowed down, the gap returned to normal.

Over and over, Angulimala tried to catch up, and every time the Buddha moved serenely on, always out of reach. Eventually, Angulimala couldn't take any more.

"Hey, you! STOP!" he yelled at the Buddha's back.

The Buddha stopped and turned, smiling innocently.

"I have stopped, Angulimala. Now it's your turn!" he called back.

"WHAAAT? What do you mean, 'I've stopped'? You're moving faster than the wind!" Angulimala shouted.

"I mean," came the reply, "I've stopped being so angry at the world that I think it owes me something. Stopped believing I can hurt enough people to make my own pain disappear. My body knows this. If you don't get it, you'll never be happy. You think your necklace will make happiness. But it won't.

"Stop running, and there's hope even for you," said the Buddha. "No matter what you've done."

Angulimala was overcome. All his pain rose up in a fury, then suddenly changed. He wept bitterly now, feeling truly awful. Finally, he took off his necklace and buried it carefully in the ground.

It would be a long time before people forgave Angulimala. He'd have to live with that. But he wanted badly to be free of the hurt he'd caused and the hurt he'd received, so he followed the Buddha out of the woods.

Think Points

As I mentioned at the beginning of this chapter, sometimes our bodies have to slow down before we can understand what's going on. Especially if we're angry or upset! It's a good idea to stop every so often, just to see where you're at.

I. What's one painful thing in your life that you'd like to put aside forever?

II. Do you experience stress or upset in your body? Where?

III. Who can you check in with about your own hurts and behaviors? This might be a friend, someone you look up to, or a therapist. Your school counselor or a teacher you trust can also help.

Build Your Own Buddha

Everyone who decides to follow the Buddhist path shares a sense that lasting peace only comes from understanding deeply what it means to be alive. It's why people still meditate in front of images of the Buddha today: to remind themselves that *it is possible* to understand and transform their lives based on that understanding. That is what the Buddha represents.

In fact, over the centuries, the act of remembering and meditating on the qualities of the original Buddha has led to many more Buddha-like figures emerging from people's imaginations. There's even a set of special figures called the *Five Buddha Mandala*, with one Buddha for each compass point, plus one at the center:

- **Eastern Buddha**—Color: *deep blue.* Associated animal: *elephant.* Top quality: *unshakeable.* Buddhist power: *totally grounded.*

- **Southern Buddha**—Color: *golden yellow.* Animal: *horse or lion.* Quality: *spiritual riches (not money!).* Power: *endless generosity.*

- **Western Buddha**—Color: *ruby red.* Animal: *peacock.* Quality: *boundless love.* Power: *deep meditation.*

- **Northern Buddha**—Color: *jungle green.* Animal: *garuda (mythical birdlike creature).* Quality: *unstoppability.* Power: *absolute fearlessness.*

- **Central Buddha**—Color: *moon white.* Animal: *dragon.* Quality: *purity of heart.* Power: *teaching truth.*

These figures are like superheroes, complete with backstories and origin tales. Your mission now: build your own Buddha!

Ground Rules

- Write, draw, or express your Buddha in any way you like.

- They're *your* thoughts and images. No one has to justify their imagination.

- Try to connect with what really inspires you or how you'd like to be.

    Let's get started!

1. What color is your Buddha? All colors are welcome!

2. Many cultures have animal guides or companions in their mythologies. What would your Buddha's associated animal be? What qualities made you choose this?

3. Would your Buddha have no gender, a specific gender, a flexible gender? Why?

4. Does your Buddha live in the east, south, west, north, or center? Why that direction?

5. Describe your Buddha's country and/or home. Perhaps it's a magic land where everyone has everything they need. Maybe they live in a badass castle! Or perhaps it's a cool, watery world or a warm desert.

6. What are your Buddha's three qualities? (See the *Five Buddha Mandala* list on page 51 for inspiration. You can have more than three!)

7. Capture whatever else is important about your Buddha. Maybe they're your own age, or old and wise. Perhaps it's how they're dressed, or their hairstyle. Remember to connect with characteristics that inspire you.

MEDITATION

Touching the Earth

This meditation can have quite a deep effect, especially when you're struggling with stress, anxiety, or just feeling that the day is getting away from you. And it's kind of a stealth meditation—no one even needs to know you are doing it.

If you can, sit outside—on a bench or on the ground. Near some trees would be ideal. If you can't get out, try and sit or lie near a window where you can see a view you like. But wherever you are, it's all good.

Body, Breath, Earth

1. Close your eyes or keep your gaze down, and let yourself be absorbed in the moment. That means:

- Check in with your body. If it's helpful, use the body scan method you learned on page 36. You're looking to be as present as you can: feet on the ground, hands at rest, relaxing as much as possible.

- Be aware of your surroundings. What are your senses bringing you? Sights, sounds, smells, touch, taste.

- Give some attention to your breathing. Whatever helps you be at ease. You can follow your breath any way you like, or do square breathing (page 11) if that feels right.

2. Notice how you're feeling. Maybe your mind is caught up in stories about stuff that's happened, as we explored earlier (page 39). See if you can acknowledge any strong feelings, and gently set aside the stories for a while.

   Ask yourself if a sense of kindness is present. If you're not sure or it feels absent, that's okay. You can still wish yourself well in your imagination or with words:

   "May I feel well in myself. May I feel better than I do. May this day bring what I need to be happy."

3. Now we're going to reach out and touch the earth. It doesn't have to be the actual earth—anything solid will do (a chair, a tree). But if you can, place your fingers or your palm on the ground or floor, beside or in front of you.

   The key here is to feel the solidity of what you are touching. Its strength. Its support.

   Keep your hand there for a minute, then try lifting it. Notice any difference? Try placing it back again. How does it feel? Do this for as long as you like.

   When you're ready, move out of meditation mode and rest easy.

   If you want to read the story behind this meditation, turn to page 96.

My First Days in the Kitchen

There I was, Katy the new girl, apprenticing at a fancy restaurant at the Blue Cliff Hotel. Their whole kitchen—tiles, surfaces, stoves—shone like the inside of a new pot.

At first, all I wanted was to be the best prep chef, best pastry cook, best sauce maker. But things change, and not always the way you expect.

Strangely, I'd always struggled around food. Feeling bad about myself, getting confused, bingeing, you know? *Eat this! Don't eat that!* I didn't even know how to decide for myself. But I knew how to cook, I liked cooking for others, and I was *good*.

There were two main chefs. They really didn't like the word *chef*.

"We're cooks!" they'd say. "Buddhist cooks, in fact!" And they'd scowl if you asked what *that* meant.

Cook Doge and Cook Yun: weirdo Buddhist cooks. I loved them. They taught me, and not just about food. When I look back on it, it's a bit like remembering a dream. I'm still not always sure I know what it all meant. But it was exciting—and fun! I kept a diary—here's a few choice excerpts of my thoughts at the time.

February 22, COOK DOGE (CD) *[cackling]: When you steam rice, Katy, look after the pot as if it's your own head! When you're washing up, treat the water as if it's your own life force.*

Nourishing your body is self-care. Take it seriously, people!

May 1, COOK YUN (CY): *When I pick up a single vege-table, I think about serving the whole world. The best way to do that is to relax, then change my life! Eat up!* These two make no sense! Awesome . . .

July 4, CD: *I was hopeless! I had to learn so much: perseverance, attention to detail, what ingredients are good, what's in season, what's not in season . . .*

Just watching them handling their knives . . . it's almost like courtesy, as if the knives were alive and really sensitive!

October 17, CY: *I used to think meditation was where it's at, this was just my job. One day I asked myself, "Everyone has a light. We never see our own. What is mine?" Then I realized: it's right here!*

Everybody's light is in their everyday life. Mine's my skills in the kitchen! But if I forget where to find this light, what's the point? Focus well for 10 minutes, then act like an idiot the rest of the day?

November 25, CD: *Don't let your thoughts and emotions get too wild or scattered. Come back to your body. That way you can take responsibility for yourself and the world.*

Those two worked 50 years together to try and get this right. I'd better listen up.

Final Entry, CD & CY: *We try to pay attention . . . In the end it's not the ingredients you cook with but the way you cook them that matters . . . We still struggle . . . Remember, Katy. You should try and surpass us!*

Think Points

I. What's the best your body has ever felt?

II. When you're learning to cook, knowing what vegetables are *"in or out of season"* matters! The same idea could be applied to all our actions in life. How do you feel when you say or do something at the wrong time or in the wrong way? What can you do about it?

III. What is your *"everyday light"*?

You Are the Teacher; Tell Us about Mindfulness

In the previous chapter, we explored how our emotions and thoughts are usually experienced in relation to our body. In this chapter, we've been looking at how our body can be a key to unlocking and understanding our ways of feeling and thinking.

In the next chapter, we'll consider some central Buddhist ideas and principles and connect how these can help us think and live more creatively. Ideas, too, are in relationship to our emotions and body. You're probably getting the picture!

Well, they say the best way to learn something is to teach it. This is usually (but not always) true. And it works for mindfulness, too. You've been meditating, reflecting on Buddhist tales, and trying out activities that can help you become more aware and positive around your emotions and your body. Let's see what you've learned by making *you* the teacher!

1. The class plan for today is to help your students learn about mindfulness. Not just the idea of it, but also what it *feels like*.

   Decide on your class size: Is it a small, concentrated lesson? Is it a big lecture hall with lots of students? Choose whatever you feel comfortable with.

2. Which meditation would you get the class to try first to give a sense of what mindfulness is? Body? Breath? Positive emotion? A combo you come up with?

   Do it yourself first, then write out the stages (see this book's meditations for examples).

   Confidence in your own experience lets you relate to others, especially if they find mindfulness hard to get their heads (and hearts) around.

3. Your students are going to write, or capture somehow, their own sense of what mindfulness is and feels like. Their job is to come up with some images or metaphors. Offer some examples of these, like:

   ● When you're with people you really love. You're just with them—absorbed for hours.

   ● A breath of fresh air.

   ● An AT-AT from Star Wars: high above the world, looking down.

   ● Patiently hand washing a shirt in a basin with soapsuds.

   ● Surfing very gracefully on a large wave.

   ● Sitting in the cool rain under a tin roof, listening to the sounds like individual thoughts and feelings coming and going.

   ● Waking up feeling contented and wishing the whole day will be like that.

You try it first! Find:

- Five metaphors of your own (for the bronze star).

- Seven metaphors (silver star).

- 10 metaphors (gold star).

Class dismissed!

Imagining Your Breath

When we explored following our breath (page 41), we learned a really important meditation in Buddhism. It might seem simple, but it sets the scene for a whole new way of learning how to pay attention to what's happening around us and respond creatively. This makes it one of the most quietly radical things you can do with your body and mind!

Now, we're going to revisit our breath, focusing this time on connecting with its extraordinary nature through our imagination.

Breathing, Being, Imagining

1. Set up well before you meditate. That means being comfortable and relaxed, checking in with your feelings. A good set of meditation habits can be encouraging, and can help you stay grounded from day to day. It's a relief not to have to do too much. Just paying attention, hanging out a little with yourself (even if you're meditating with others).

   Find your way to arrive and settle. Wish yourself well as you begin.

2. Let's establish a connection to our present experience by following our breathing for a few minutes, marking each breath with a silent count. You can count before or after each breath. Try both ways and see what you prefer:

Count 1, breathe in, breathe out. Count 2, breathe in, breathe out.

Breathe in, breathe out, count 1. Breathe in, breathe out, count 2.

Do this in cycles of 10. Whenever your mind wanders off, come back to your body, rest easy, and begin again at 1 . . .

3. When you're ready, drop the counting and try to track the flow of your breath, from the moment it first comes into your body till the moment it leaves.

Your breath is doing a job: nourishing you with oxygen, bringing you life. Imagine each cell in your body alive with goodness, like the cells in a honeycomb, rich with honey.

As you breathe, notice your other senses.

- What does your breath sound like?

- Where do you feel it most inside your body?

- Is it warming, cooling, or both?

- When you breathe through your nose, do you catch any scents or smells?

- Do you prefer breathing through your nose or mouth?

- Do you like breathing with your eyes open or closed?

4. Find an image that works for you to connect with the richness of your breath. Try imagining it as the ocean, coming in and going out. Maybe it's like hearing the wind in the trees.

Feel free to improvise, play, and be intuitive with this for as long as you like. Then, finish and let the experience soak in for a while.

CHAPTER 3

Making a World
with Your Mind

The stories we tell to make sense of things matter. We share them all the time (hello, social media!). And what we take in or put out there has a big effect—on us and on the world we know.

The Buddha thought this was crucial: How we experience the world is based on how we engage with it. If we're angry, society is an unsafe space. If we're chill, we cope much better. We can't control other people's behavior, only how we think about and carry things in our mind. Our happiness literally depends on it.

That's a radical thought: We take part in making the reality we live through *with our mind*, every moment of every day. It's a big responsibility! It's also hopeful: change is always possible.

Buddhist ideas like this won't just boost what you learn in school; they can also revolutionize how you get along with other people and your whole outlook on life. Read on wisely!

Waking Up Different

That "prince" we keep meeting . . . definitely not a prince anymore. There was something about him, though. Sitting with his back against the tree, he looked pretty good: upright, calm, concentrated but relaxed. Not bad for someone who'd recently been at death's door.

When we last checked in, he was remembering his childhood and a moment when he'd been at peace: sitting under a tree, just breathing. Now, here he was, changed beyond recognition from that boy, yet also familiar—following a thread he'd been holding his whole life. Who was he now?

Later, he'd describe what happened next as diving into his own body, heart, and mind—riding quiet, steady waves of breath into a new space that *felt* like understanding something important for the first time. Like the moon coming out from behind the clouds at night. There it was, shining above him in the dark. His eyes were closed, looking inside.

In a way, suddenly it all seemed simple. First his breath, like an old friend he'd forgotten, now back with him. Then, how he felt about his life, connecting with the best of himself, whatever had helped him get through it all. For the rest of what he'd understood, no words can do justice to the experience and the mystery:

Everything is connected, rising and passing away, just like our breath. The whole universe breathing in and out, life beginning, ending, beginning again. All so complex, so detailed, impossible to know completely.

We can't control it all. Everyone thinks they are at the center of it, but nobody really is. That's frightening. But if, over time, you sit still with your own struggle, confusion, pain, hate, longing—eventually you realize that it's just as hard for everybody else. This feels like love beginning: It wells up naturally in response.

You notice all this more, playing out in cycles, rising and passing away, moment to moment, day to day, year to year. And you stop resisting, let go, catch the rhythm like music or a dance or your heartbeat. And, gradually, you feel free to really take part in life . . .

Something special happened that night. Someone's mind opened like a tightly closed hand gradually unfolding, holding a gift inside. A leaf, a shell, a jewel.

The cool night air brushed their cheek. Now they knew who they were. The Buddha's eyes opened:

"I'm awake! And anyone can do this . . ."

Think Points

Change can be scary and full of possibilities at the same time. We can change our hair, our look, our crushes, our friends, our name. We grow older, start over in a new school, new town. Do we ever stop being who we were?

I. What changes have you made in your life that helped you feel more confident about your place in the world? What other changes have you thought about making?

II. Buddha literally means "someone who's woken up to how things are." What do you wish people would *wake up to* in the world? Why don't they?

III. If you imagine your closed hand opening with a gift for someone you love, and someone you don't, what would it be?

ACTIVITY

Mind Journaling

Some ancient writers from China and Greece, at roughly the same time in history as the Buddha, thought all wisdom and learning was captured in just two words: *"Know yourself."*

Good advice! The only place you can start on any journey of discovery is where you currently are. The tricky part, of course, is *"knowing."*

As we've seen in our meditations, you can know something through your body. Obviously, you can know it with your mind. You can also know it—feel it—in your heart. For true understanding, you need all three.

To get a sense of what's going on for you, try keeping two mind journals for a week, recording:

1. Your dreams or first thoughts as you wake.

2. Your activity online: scrolling, posting, messaging, commenting, etc.

You can capture this however you like: words or pictures, audio or video. You don't need a complete record, just key moments, aspects, or feelings that come up for you. Like this:

- *Dream: A large shaggy dog was chasing me! I was scared, but then it turned out to be friendly . . . Then it turned into my teacher! Woke up laughing . . .*

- *Online: Sent a message to Jamal. Apologized about yesterday. Still feeling mad about it, but I shouldn't have said that. I'm worried he's still mad at me. Ended up doomscrolling for an hour . . .*

1. Morning

- Keep your journal near your bed. When you wake, make an entry right away. If you can't remember your dream, record your first thoughts, whatever's on your mind. No need to edit yourself if you can help it. Just whatever comes out . . .

- If you're writing, it's interesting to try this using your nondominant hand. What does it feel like to not have your usual physical ability?

- Be aware of your body. Imagine where your dreams or thoughts live in your body. Also, how do you feel?

2. Evening

- Before you go to sleep, take some time to note your online activity. Use the same method as in the morning, or mix it up.

- Asking yourself how things feel emotionally and in your body can be revealing! Were you tense recording that video earlier? How did that "like" make you feel?

- No need to share online. Keep this experience as secret wisdom for yourself.

At the end of the week, read, listen, or watch it all back. Try again in a month. See what you make of it. Any themes? Has anything changed?

The Way Things Are

Remember our theme this chapter: If we're at ease, a lot of what we *experience* in the world gets easier, too.

We'll do this meditation in four stages. Anywhere is fine, in whatever position's comfortable for you.

Letting Go into the Flow

1. Connect with your breath. Let it guide you toward relaxing deeply, letting go of any body tension you notice. Give yourself permission to be just as you are today. You're worth the space you occupy:
    May I be well in myself. May I get the most out of this . . .

2. Notice what's coming in through your senses:

    - *Light or color through closed or open eyelids*

    - *Scents on the air or tastes in your mouth*

    - *The weight of your hands resting on your lap*

    - *What sounds can you hear?*

    Bring to mind something you find challenging in your life. Notice how you feel about it—and wish yourself well again.

    Try not to get caught up in any story around this. You can keep your attention wider by coming back to your senses and how your body feels.

3. Start paying attention to the flow of things. Like this:

    - *How sounds rise and fall away: traffic passing, distant voices moving*

    - *Bodily sensations (aches, twinges, itches) that change if you move mindfully*

    - *Wind blowing through trees*

- *Scents coming and going*

- *Clouds drifting across the sky*

Breathe normally, as easily as you can. Relax into your awareness of everything changing, rising, passing.

4. Take your attention to the crown of your head. Now, be aware of the sky above: its great expanse, all around to the horizons. Try to get a sense of its space in your mind.

    It's time to let go of the difficulty you noticed earlier. Imagine just letting it rise into the sky. Perhaps passing through a ray of light between your crown and the sky, or just drifting up and away to dissolve.

    Take your attention to your feet on the floor or ground. Imagine how solid and strong the earth is below. Try and get a sense of how deep it goes: miles of support under you.

    Again, let go of your struggles for a moment—perhaps they are passing into the earth as if you have roots. Or maybe they are gradually being absorbed into the rich soil, dissolving into rocks that are millions of years old.

When you are ready, let go of this meditation, too, and rest easy.

Dragon Fire

Her strongest memory: rafts on fire floating downriver in the infinite, ink-black night, sparks rising and passing beyond sight into the dark, welcoming sky. Kassie stood on the bank, watching.

One week before, the Stranger had started coming to her dreams. She simply wandered into Kassie's mind every evening, shared a meal, hung out. When Kassie woke, it felt as if they'd been talking all night: about life, about wisdom. That was Kassie's main deal—she wanted people to know she was smart, to recognize her as a born leader. She would follow no one.

After these intense dream meetings, Kassie could feel her mind wanting to bloom and burst into day with new ideas. She wanted to tell her sisters, but something held her back. These thoughts that she was on fire with might not be her own, and that scorched her. She had been determined her whole life to be an original thinker: Kassie the Cleverest, who burns brightest of all.

In some ways, she wasn't wrong. She and her sisters *were* the leaders of the future. And they scorned the leaders now, who burned with pride in all the wrong ways: *"We know best. We are the holders of truth. We will keep you safe."* Only, the world that resulted did not seem true to her. Violence was never far away. People who mattered were ignored. Wealth was not shared evenly. The rules seemed stacked against any change. Kassie felt conflicted. She could take part in all that, if she chose to. Yet, she burned differently.

She lay down, smoldering in the dark. The Stranger was there again, walking in the yard outside. Kassie followed her beneath a bright moon. She saw the Stranger go into a woodshed. Kassie went to the window. Inside, the Stranger was sitting perfectly quiet, perfectly still. Her eyes were closed, and it seemed that she breathed out night itself.

Suddenly, a great dragon uncoiled itself from around the inside walls. It had been there all along, like part of the fabric of the place. Kassie watched, mesmerized, horrified, unable to move as it rose up around the Stranger and breathed—not night, but fire. Yet when the flames died down, the dragon was gone. The Stranger faced Kassie, her eyes open, unharmed:

"Kassie, the dragon is absorbed. Bring everything you know: We'll send it on fire shrines down the river. Let this be your offering to the future. If you want to lead, learn how to be uncertain."

Later, Kassie told her sisters about her dreams, the Stranger, the dragon, and the rafts. Then she listened to them, carefully. They would all lead one day. They were getting ready.

Think Points

When you start paying attention, you notice what's feeding your mind as it runs away with itself. Pride can be healthy or not. So can ambition. We can learn the difference.

I. Some people are quite sure of themselves. Some are very unsure. Where do you fall in the spectrum?

II. What are you most curious about at the moment?

III. If you could set fire to three ideas, which would you choose and why?

Spending Time with Reality

If you were to ask 100 Buddhists to break Buddhism down to a core idea, my guess is you'd hear an even spread across:

- Mindfulness

- Kindness or nonviolence

- Everything is interconnected

There are lots of other good answers, but these might be the main three. You've hopefully caught a glimpse of them already in our meditations and stories. In chapter 4, we'll be focusing on how you can live non-violently as you make your way through the world. But here we're going to pay attention to being interconnected.

Almost the first thing the Buddha observed on "waking up" was this: Reality is super complex and everything is connected. That means everything—I mean *everything*—in the entire universe is constantly rising and falling, coming into being and passing out again. Sometimes slowly, sometimes quickly. And it all depends on whatever impossible-to-predict web of supports and conditions happens to be in play at any moment.

Now, since everything's also subtly changing all the time, this means, in reality, that everything's always in motion, in flux. Nothing's fixed forever. And that includes *us*. This is why it matters to Buddhists: we, too, can change.

You've maybe heard someone who's amazingly good at what they do (an athlete, artist, scientist) talk about "being in the zone." That's what we're going to try to get a feel for as we take a walk or roll around reality.

1. You can do this anywhere in 10 minutes, including indoors. If you can find an hour somewhere in nature (a garden or park in your neighborhood), even better.

Just move as normal, except that you have one goal: to notice carefully anything arising and passing away in connection to something else. For example:

- The wind blows and your hair moves.

- A leaf falls from a tree and you turn your head.

- Your motion disturbs a stick or a bird.

- Your breath gets heavier as you walk/roll.

- Someone yells and you feel alert.

- The grass crumples under your wheels/feet.

- The rain starts. One drop lands on the back of your head. You speed up.

2. Notice simple connections or more complex chains of events. Stop every so often, if you can, and close your eyes.

   Your inner experience is shaped by your environment. How you view the world is affected by your state of mind. How are you feeling? How's your body doing? Keep going . . .

When you get home, sit quietly for a few minutes and let the experience soak in.

Try to plan space for this activity regularly for a week. Record your impressions: the things that caught your attention.

A Sense of Perspective

Change is a hopeful possibility, but sometimes it's so hard to believe it. Especially about ourselves.

Buddhism has many useful perspectives on the times we feel stuck, trapped by our own habits. One important approach separates what makes up a human being into five areas:

- Form (body)

- Sensations/feeling (what you take in with your senses and whether it's pleasant, unpleasant, or neutral)

- Perception (how you understand and label things: *Baby! Pink! Happy!*)

- Habits of body, speech, or mind (how you act in response to things)

- Consciousness (all of the above going on, all the time, building a sense of ourselves and the world)

Everyone's like a changing "bundle" of these aspects. It *seems* personal, and we *feel* fixed, but we're not! Anytime you feel stuck, try this simple meditation.

Untying the Bundle

1. Start with who you are now. You may want to change some things in your life, but you don't need to be a different person to meditate today. Meditate as you. You are valid.

    As always, this means:

    - Check in with your body, sit or lie comfortably, breathe easy, and give yourself permission to relax.

- Notice how you feel. Take time to respect it.

- Wish yourself well: remember a good time or try to find your own encouraging words.

2. For this meditation, try picturing your ideal landscape. Maybe it's right where you are. Perhaps a spring meadow. Or in the high mountains. Whatever inspires you.

   Imagine being there. What's the weather like? Are there birds? Are you alone or with others? Anything else?

   Bask in the space. It's okay to enjoy how you'd like to experience the world. Allow yourself to be as relaxed as you can.

3. Remember the thing about being a bundle of different aspects? A body with a name, mind, and heart that thinks, feels, sorts out the world? Familiar likes and dislikes, fears and loves?

   Try imagining yourself as a bundle of wheat or grass. It's strange, but give it a go! Picture it in your mind. You're loosely held together with something: a colored ribbon *(what color?)*, some simple twine. Maybe your bundle's all thick or fine stalks, maybe a mix.

   You're standing in the sunshine. The sky above is blue. Someone friendly comes along and finds your bundle. They pull gently on the binding—and *whoosh* . . .

   The bundle comes undone. What's that like?

   Just sit in the space. Breathe deep and easy till it's time to stop meditating.

Two Silences

The king always wanted the best of anything: best palaces, best chariots, best food. In his favor, he also greatly valued learning. Naturally, he had the best advisers available.

At the time, Buddhism was back in fashion.

"I know the Buddhist basics already," he declared airily to his advisers. "Ethics, meditation, wisdom. *Everybody* learns that.

"What I'd like is something even better. Something truly wise."

Soon enough, they came before him with a story:

Once, Your Majesty, there was a king like you. His father had known the Buddha, and he wanted to meet the great teacher himself. The king's doctor sometimes cared for anyone who was sick in the Buddhist community, and he agreed to take the king to where the Buddha was meditating in a forest with over 1,000 friends.

They rode, then walked, for hours. It was getting very late, very dark. The king got very nervous:

"Is this a trap? Where are you taking me? You said we were near, but I don't hear a sound! How can 1,000 people make no noise?"

The doctor smiled and led him on. Suddenly, they emerged into a giant clearing and, sure enough, there was a huge crowd of meditators, sitting as still as stones.

The king was dumbstruck.

"How can this be?" he exclaimed.

No one stirred. But the Buddha's eyes opened and met the king's. Then, silently, the Buddha held up a single golden flower.

"This, sire, was the deepest teaching."

His advisers bowed serenely. The king lost his mind!

"Silence? Flowers? That's your *best*?"

Terrified, they huddled until one spoke up anxiously:

"There is one man. He's often called the best of the mountain teachers, but he won't come . . ."

"We'll see about that," the king replied, ominously.

The next week, down from the mountain came the teacher, looking to buy provisions. And shall we just say, he was *diverted* to the palace?

The king had assembled everyone: courtiers, advisers, family, friends, hangers-on. The teacher was old and walked slowly past their ranks in the great hall. He climbed painstakingly up to the magnificent lectern provided for this greatest teaching of their lives.

He surveyed them for a full minute. Then, seizing the lectern with both hands and, with surprising strength, he rattled it so loud and long that the racket echoed off the palace walls.

Then, he spoke into the silence: "I've given you the *best* teaching. *All of it.*"

And he walked back out the way he came, no one daring to stop him.

Think Points

When we don't get what we expect, it can feel like a challenge to our whole way of experiencing the world. What to do about that is the puzzle Buddhism sets out to solve. Some answers will need lots of space—and a lot less talking. Listen . . .

I. When you don't have the words to explain something that feels important to you, what do you do?

II. If you had to give up one of three senses for a day—sight, hearing, or speech—which would you choose? Why?

III. How long do you think you could be silent for? A minute, five minutes, an hour? Prove it!

E.M.W.

One of the earliest maps of the Buddhist path seems very simple: *Ethics, Meditation, Wisdom* (E.M.W.). Easy, right? Well, each of these is like a whole, expanding universe.

In Buddhism, ethics means something like *"Guidelines that help us learn how to behave in ways that support everyone's well-being (including our own) for the long term."*

You'll need to dig out that mandala map of relationships you made in chapter 1 (page 26) for reference. For this exercise, create a new page or document, expressed any way you like—written, drawn, or using a device.

1. Start by defining each category (ethics, meditation, wisdom) in a broad way. What does each mean to you? Like this:

   • *Ethics: Don't be sketchy.*

   • *Meditation: Learn to chill out.*

   • *Wisdom: Real smart, not fake smart.*

2. Let's get more detailed. The Buddhist path suggests paying attention in three areas: *body, speech,* and *mind*. So, most Buddhists would take on five general *dos and don'ts* for ethics, like:

   Body

   • *Only act in kind ways. | Don't cause harm.*

   • *Be generous when you can. | Don't take what isn't yours.*

   • *In relationships, go for happiness more than constant drama, and learn about consent. | Don't cause psychological or sexual harm (you can research what this means by looking online or talking to a school counselor or trusted adult).*

Speech

- *Practice truthful communication.* | *Try not to lie about stuff.*

Mind

- *Live with as much awareness as you can.* | *Don't do things that make you feel more confused.*

Using this framework of *body, speech, and mind*, come up with at least one *do* and *don't* of your own for ethics, meditation, and wisdom. You might start with what you can do personally to build your skills in all three areas. For example:

Ethics

- Volunteer some time to help a friend or a good cause. *(Body)*

- Try not to say anything negative for a whole day. *(Speech)*

Meditation

- Meditate once a week. *(Mind)*

- Stop rushing everywhere! Take more time to do things well. *(Body/Mind)*

Wisdom

- Ask people older than me to tell their stories about things that matter—love, childhood, ambition, fear, death, etc. *(Speech/Mind)*

- Take a break from screens or being online for a weekend. See if this changes my emotional experience. *(Mind)*

3. Sort people from your relationship mandala into each of the categories (ethics, meditation, wisdom). Note why you put them there. Place yourself in the category that is your strongest area.

When you're done, keep this with your relationship mandala for future reference.

Imagining Your Best

In this meditation, we'll lean into the possibilities for positive change that you already carry inside you. The Buddhist tradition is clear that all beings have something inside, however hidden, that can connect to dignity. This meditation is a good antidote for those days when you have trouble seeing your own potential.

You can find your own best way to do this, making sure you feel physically comfortable and well supported as you begin.

Being with Your Potential

1. Spend a couple of minutes just taking in how you're doing.

   - How's your body feeling? Easy and relaxed? Stiff or sore? Try to use your breath to soften any tension you're holding.

   - How's your emotional weather? Stormy? Occasional gloom? The sun coming out? Just notice lightly. Remember, the weather eventually clears up.

   - How's your mind? Busy, full, and active? Sleepy and quiet? Calm and still? Again, just noticing is good. You don't have to stop thinking to meditate. Your mind will get quiet when it's ready.

2. Here's the familiar reminder to wish yourself well. Start simple. You can use words to send yourself some good vibes, or you can find a memory or wish that catches the same feeling:
   May the best version of me never be far away . . .

3. Now, we'll add a twist. Using your imagination, see if you can come up with an image or scene that captures your own sense of potential.
   To help, first meditate for a while on each of these scenarios from the Buddhist tradition. It's okay to open your eyes and read them if you can't remember. Really let them soak into your mind:

- *You find some honey in a cave abandoned by bees. It's sweet, mellow, and delicious. You can eat it—or give it away . . .*

- *Some gold was buried in a field. You come along and find it . . .*

- *You're holding the mold for a statue. On the outside, it's plain. But when you break it open, there's a beautiful face inside . . .*

See what you can come up with. Like:

- *Making that perfect shot at basketball . . .*

- *The birthday cake you baked turning out perfectly . . .*

- *Fixing some code or writing a cool app for the first time . . .*

When you end the meditation, note what you imagined. This is *your* treasure.

The Elephant

They called me *the Elephant*. We all got good names back then: *Frankie the Fish, Carlo the Crocodile, Mickey the Mule*. Why *Elephant*? Because elephants never forget. I never forgot no one I met in the neighborhood.

There were these five guys who hung out at my boss's bar. And boy, could they argue! They never stopped, day or night:

"There's no such thing as heaven or hell. You die, then there's just nothin'."

"You sayin' my poor dead mother is nothin'?"

"There's gotta be life on other planets."

"Well, I hope when them aliens come, they take you first!"

Argue, argue, argue. It kinda grated on your nerves after a while. My boss took me aside:

"Ernie," he says, "take care of this. One way or the other, they gotta shut up!"

I had an idea. They were so sure of themselves: read the news, gave lectures at the dinner table, never saw no one rolling their eyes! Well, what if they couldn't see nothing at all?

"You guys," I says, "you think you're smart. But I bet I could fool you so easy."

Straightaways, every one of them starts boasting like he knows everything better than *anyone*. Then they get mad at each other, so we have to break up a brawl.

"Okay, here's the deal. If I can't fool you, each one of you boys drinks free for a year."

Dollar signs in their eyes.

"But if I do . . . you never set foot in here again with your malarkey."

They were cocky as roosters. I made some phone calls. My boss watched nervously: I don't think it's what he had in mind.

Out back, there's five cars, five friendly drivers—and five guys suddenly quieter than usual.

"Get in!" I says, "Just a short ride. But we gotta blindfold ya first."

For some reason this bothered them.

"Ah, stop sweatin'. I ain't gonna throw you in the river."

When they got out at the warehouse, they were real confused.

"Time for a game," I says.

We had an old garbage truck there, all beat up, but it still ran pretty good. One by one, I took each of the guys to stand by the truck. I put his hand on one part of it only, then asked him what it was.

The first got a mudflap over a wheel. He yells out: *"It's a rhinoceros' ear!"*

The second got a fuel cable. He screams: *"It's a python!"*

The third got a tow rope. He faints! *"A hangman's noose!"*

The fourth got a piston: *"The barrel of a gun!"*

The fifth touched the side of the truck. I thought he'd get it, but he just sobs: *"Don't put me up against the wall."*

I heard they all stopped arguing so much after that. Another win for *the Elephant*!

Think Points

Everyone thinks they're right, but being right doesn't equal understanding. Spend too much time arguing, and soon you'll find threats everywhere . . .

I. What do you usually do when you feel confused? Talk? Distract yourself? Get upset? Meditate?

II. Are you the kind of person who likes a good argument or debate? Do you think positive or harmonious disagreement is possible?

III. What would being coolheaded in the moment be like for you?

Remix Time

The Buddha happily recycled and reimagined the language, myths, and stories they learned to make a set of new, creatively original teachings that expressed what they'd come to understand.

It's a bit like sampling in music: You take an old song—just a tiny part—loop, change, or add a beat . . . and bang! A new piece of musical magic is born.

A good example of this kind of process concerns one of the most famous Buddhist teachings, usually known as the *Four Noble Truths*.

This list might have been based on an ancient Indian medicine formula, like a doctor's diagnosis and prescription when someone's sick:

The Four Noble Truths as Medicine

1. The truth that all life can experience suffering (*diagnosis—working out what's wrong*)

2. The truth that suffering has causes we can recognize (*identifying the cause of the illness*)

3. The truth that suffering can come to an end (*identifying what the cure would be*)

4. The truth that there's a path we can follow to ease, and even end, our own suffering (*prescribing a recommended treatment*)

We can't be sure if medicine really was the model for the Buddha's teaching, but it makes sense.

Today, you're going to make your own remix!

1. List all the things in your life that feel like suffering—big or small. These could be:

   Bullying at school. Fights in my family. Pressure to get good grades. Anxiety and stress. Acne. My sports team sucks! Bands never play near our town.

2. What do you think causes your suffering? For example:
Other people! I'm really sensitive. My parents don't understand. I hate my teacher. We live in the middle of nowhere.

3. What might help change things? For example:
Talking to friends, people I trust. Doing meditations that help me feel better. I need more personal space! Going to college near a big city.

4. Come up with a simple version of the Four Noble Truths for someone younger than you, under 10. Like:

   i.   *Suffering*: Sometimes we don't feel good.

   ii. *Cause of suffering*: Often, it's when we don't get what we think we want or don't like what's happening.

   iii. *Ending of suffering*: You can do something about it, even when you think you can't.

   iv. *Path to end suffering*: Be curious about what's going on in your body, mind, and feelings. Be kind and generous to yourself and others—it'll help!

Get someone else to do this, too, and compare remixes.

Mind the Gap

Sometimes we can feel as if we're just going round and round—the same uncertainties, anxieties, fears, angers, loves, and hates—like we're stuck on a hamster wheel in a bad place, going nowhere fast.

Buddhism teaches that you can learn to avoid these painful cycles; you can step off the wheel. The trick is to notice and spend time in the "gap" between when your mind receives information through your senses (seeing, hearing, smelling, tasting, touching *something*) and what happens next (usually a reaction: *I like it, I want it! I don't like it, I don't want it!*).

If you can stay aware in this gap, instead of *reacting*, you can pause, assess calmly and kindly, and then *respond* creatively. Let's give it a try.

Finding the Space to Be Skillful

1. Make sure you're comfortable. While you settle, check in with your breath as it comes and goes.

   Decide to use this time well. Trust yourself. Wish yourself the best with words, wishes, or memories—whatever works for you.

2. Call to mind any struggles you have going on. Where do they live in your body? Notice any tension in your hands, belly, chest, back, head, or shoulders. Imagine breathing into it and letting the tension go.

   - Pay attention to your thoughts as they bubble up. Notice if there's any sense of going round and round in a story or thoughts piling up, one after the other.

   - Imagine breathing into any story or thought-tangle—and just gently blowing it away, like shooing away a small rain cloud.

3. Try to relax into watching your mind. It's a challenge, watching with *just* the right kind of light attention. The way you might

concentrate on staying in the flow in a video game. Not too tight, not too loose . . .

- Notice any space between thoughts. Now pause . . . no need to judge yourself—it's tricky! Keep trying. Notice and pause, notice and pause.

4. Do the same with your emotions. Notice any little flare-ups of feeling.

- Again, just notice and pause. No judgment if you get carried away. Come back, relax, and try to get into the game.

5. Take a break every so often, then play more. Like most games, the more you practice, the easier it gets. Try and get a sense of that space in your mind between each thought and feeling.

   Look for it throughout your day after meditation. And, when you remember, press pause . . .

Meg and the Heart's Release

"Meg! Meg! Oh, where has she got to now?"

They'd been traveling cross-country for 13 weeks. Mother and daughter, living out of an old van, homeschooling. #VanLife, supposedly. It didn't feel like an adventure today.

Meg came running. She was the greatest comfort of Maya's life—also a 12-year-old tearaway who could sniff out trouble at a thousand yards.

"Mom! I found a peach orchard. The best trees! They're not in season, so no one's there. Can I go?"

Maya frowned. "I don't know, Meg, maybe going on your own isn't for the best."

"But it's safe! I can handle myself. Just for the morning . . ."

"Look, I know you're capable. I just don't think it's smart to be there alone."

"I can *handle* it. I just need some downtime—from all of *this* . . ."

That was a low blow. Maya understood.

"Meg," she said, drawing a long breath, "you do what you think it's time for, okay? But meet me back here at 12. Deal?"

"Deal!" Meg was delighted, and raced off.

The peach grove was gorgeous. She found the perfect tree to sit under. Sunlight dimpled her face. Green leaves and green, new-forming fruit made it like a dream.

Only, Meg was restless. She couldn't find *quite* the right spot to sit comfortably. The ground was all gnarly with roots.

Soon her mind turned to darker thoughts. She was fed up being hungry and dirty. Resentment flared up. She daydreamed about getting revenge on someone—*anyone*. In five minutes, her head was a mess!

Suddenly, she snapped out of it. "What am I *doing*?" And, genuinely spooked, she hightailed it out of the orchard, running hard back to the van.

"Mom, it was terrible!" Meg cried, panting. "I *couldn't* handle it!"

Maya listened, wiping Meg's tears away carefully. She said:

"While you and your mind are growing, Meg, sometimes you just can't fly solo. I still struggle with that . . . but I'll tell you five things that helped me:

"First is good friends you can rely on. Kind friends, with values you share.

"Second is figuring out how to live up to *your own* values. And the kind of person you *don't* want to become.

"Third, get to know yourself. Learn about your mind. Talk to folks about that side of your education.

"Fourth, persevere! Persist. Don't let anyone tell you that you *can't* understand, especially when you don't.

"And fifth, get comfortable with the flow of life. You can't turn back the tides, but you can surf the waves. You don't have to be bigger than life—just try to let go into it.

"That's how your heart gets released from whatever happened in the peach grove."

Maya ruffled her daughter's hair, then they headed off together into town.

Think Points

People spend their whole lives maturing. It's not long enough! Sometimes you just have to follow your nose and make sure you learn from where it leads you.

I. Would you say you're too independent, not independent enough, or a good balance?

II. Write down three things about school you can handle—and three you can't.

III. What helps when you can't handle something?

ACTIVITY

A Bird's-Eye View of Your Mind

One of the most important breakdowns of the Buddhist approach to life is known as the *Noble Eightfold Path.* It's presented as the complete package, and we'll go into that aspect more fully in the next chapter. Here, we're going to focus on the stages that concern our mind.

1. Make time to read this complete sequence of stages of the path, *including explanations after each stage about how it relates to our mind, speech, or body*:

The Noble Eightfold Path

"Right" here means: *helpful, clear, skilled, honed, perfected.*

    i.   **Right Understanding:** *Knowing that everything's interconnected as part of the flowing nature of life. Actions have consequences; nothing lasts forever.*

    ii.   **Right Intention:** *Being clear about how you want to live and what will encourage you to follow through.*

    iii.   **Right Speech:** *Speaking truthfully, kindly, and harmoniously—at the right time.*

    iv.   **Right Action:** *Behaving in a skillful, ethical way; not harming yourself or others.*

    v.   **Right Livelihood:** *Earning your living in a way that doesn't cause suffering or harm to yourself or others.*

    vi.   **Right Effort:** *Putting your time and energy into things that help you live up to your values and ideals (for example, practicing meditation to cultivate a calm mind and develop positive emotions).*

    vii.   **Right Mindfulness:** *Remembering what you've learned. You're not fixed, and there's a way to be in the flow, in the moment, that strengthens your mind (living in that "gap" we explored on page 86).*

    viii.   **Right Concentration:** *Developing your ability to focus in meditation so you can go deeper into it; learning how to spend more time in a positive mental space.*

2. Come up with your own explanation of each of the stages to do with your mind:

   i.   Identify which stages you think are connected to the mind. It might help to remove all those from your list that don't seem relevant.

   ii.   You've seen the explanations above. Make your own headings, and freestyle about what the words mean to you, such as:

   Understanding: What I think I know!
   Mindfulness: This is hard! I am pretty scattered, but sometimes I can get in the zone.
   Concentration: I can focus, but I find imagining stuff weird. I like to concentrate on something solid that seems real. Meditation helps me with studying.

3. Once you have a set of versions of your own, rearrange them into any order you think works best. Note why you chose that order.

   You now have your own mind path: follow it!

MEDITATION

Positive Spirals

Once you've discovered the space between feeling something and reacting to it, Buddhism lays out a whole different possibility for your mind: you're not on a wheel—now you're riding a *spiral*!

Spirals are everywhere: the inside of a shell, the thread of a screw, a strand of DNA. Go find some examples of spirals, then try this "meditation spiral."

Getting Creative

1. Once you're comfortable, follow your breathing as it rises and falls.

   Imagine a beautiful light or dark blue sky overhead. Imagine yourself in the blue sky, floating happily.

2. The sky's a good place to start with the spiral. You might not feel great right now—that's okay. What we'll do is meditate on the possibility of positive states rising in us. Connect with them in imagination, but in a grounded way.

   The first one is just us being a positive force in the world.

   Recall a time you made a really good decision that affected you or other people well. Maybe in your family. Maybe with your friends. Something you did that was appreciated or you were proud of. How did it feel? What happens in your body, heart, and mind when you remember?

3. Next, let's connect with the idea of feeling alive, happy, and free.

   It's like finally being able to go out again after you've been grounded. Or the summer holidays rolling around. Or if you love school, presenting a project and relishing your chance to shine! See if you can let your mind rest with that kind of experience.

4. Rising further, let's imagine life just being really calm and safe in the background. Like there's a deep well you can draw on, even when difficult things happen.

   If you haven't had that experience in your life yet, imagine gently what it might be like. Probably all the older people you know thought they'd never cut it as an adult, but most manage, most of the time. They love, work, have friends, do many invisible kind-nesses every year. And so will you.

5. Finally, the bit of the spiral that means you are in the zone, connected to how things flow, feeling good about being part of it all. See if you can connect to this feeling of how well you can do

things sometimes—how capable you are, maybe in ways people don't see. That's okay, it still counts.

6. Spend as long as you like on each part before you stop. How has this affected the way you are feeling?

CHAPTER 4

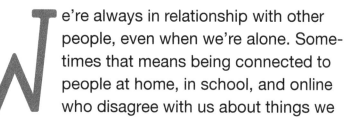

Giving Your Gifts to the Universe

We're always in relationship with other people, even when we're alone. Sometimes that means being connected to people at home, in school, and online who disagree with us about things we believe really matter: equality, injustice, the environment, how our country is run, war, a thousand issues . . .

How can we take our place in society with any confidence? As you meet the world, it helps to build up resources of compassion and mindfulness so you can cope and manage stress around the challenges that lie ahead. The right tools will enable you to flourish and engage consciously with the welfare of those you love and the future of this fragile planet.

Buddhism encourages us to live in a way that causes as little harm as possible. The stories, activities, and meditations here lay the groundwork for a sense of community you can contribute to in that spirit. You've got this! Come share your gifts . . .

The Goddess and the Serpent

Imagine your whole life you'd been a prince, raised to be above everyone, different. Then, a game changer: You discover a secret that could change the world. What would you do? Keep it to yourself or go tell someone *now*?

The Buddha was still sitting under the tree and genuinely wasn't sure. There was no more "prince," no more loneliness, no more grief. But understanding how reality works doesn't mean you know *everything*. Only what matters.

Still, it was so peaceful just sitting there! Why wouldn't anyone stay away from the big, bad world if they could? And yet, there it was again. That insistent little voice that kept whispering through leaves:

"You should share this."

The Buddha knew that other people could understand, too. Not everyone, at least not immediately, but some folks were ready. They would soak in the truth the way the roots of a lily pad can draw strength from the rich mud at the bottom of a pond. They were the buds floating on the surface—ripe to burst open in the sun.

Flowers filled the Buddha's mind. Again, so peaceful . . . again, that voice:

"Share it . . ."

Now another thought came in:

"Okay, you've got it now. Enjoy. No one wants a lecture from you. There's plenty of that already in the world. Aren't you just making yourself 'special' again? What gives you the right?"

The Buddha smiled, recognizing this doubting voice like an old friend come to say goodbye. Then, he instinctively reached out, placing one hand on the soft moss and cool earth next to the roots of the tree that had offered shelter and shade for days now. And, suddenly, there she was:

It was as if she was made of trees. She was old and strong and beautiful, like winter branches against snow when the year turns. Then she smiled, as young as spring blossoms in a freshening rain. Now, she laughed like a cascade of green leaves rustling in the summer wind. She waited, nut brown as fine boughs in fall, her hair adorned with all the gold-red colors of the sun.

And there was a giant serpent beside her—the king of the cobras. He did not threaten her, but instead circled the tree where the Buddha sat, then rose up to his full height—his magnificent hood spread like protection from any storm that could come—and took his place behind the Buddha's head.

Now, they spoke together with one voice, the goddess of the earth and the oldest creature to come out of the sea:

"We will always protect you. Share what you have been given. You are ready."

Think Points

We all need guidance from others to make a lasting difference. We also need to find our own spark of inspiration inside. Integrating the two is like magic: It keeps us right, and so much becomes possible . . .

I. What three gifts of experience could you share? *(Things you've learned that it would help most people to know.)*

II. How resourced do you feel to cope with your problems? What do you need?

III. Who would you rather have as your protector: the goddess or the serpent? Why?

Map Your Community of Hope

Everyone knows what fear feels like. Everyone recognizes hope (even when it feels impossible or far off). So, as you move through society, it's worth paying attention to your own fears and hopes and how they are connected. That way, you can catch fear when it's driving your reactions and find a way forward in the dark.

When you're feeling afraid, the Buddha suggests something like this:

- Notice it, then keep doing what you're doing.

- Try noticing *without* judgment and *with* kindness.

- Learn to stay in the present moment; don't focus too much on the past or future.

- The only way forward is to be deeply honest with yourself about what's happening for you, paying attention in the way the Buddhist path suggests.

Hope happens when you live this way. It won't fix everything, but it can ease your mind if you ever feel paralyzed with a kind of horrified anxiety at the state of the world. Most importantly, hope comes when you realize you don't need to—can't—go it alone.

Remember the structure of the Cultivating Kindness meditation (page 7)? We're going to use it to draw a map of what hope looks like for you in the shape of other people.

1. Note these four categories:

- Your friends

- Acquaintances and strangers

- People you find difficult

- Everyone else

Draw, write out, or record *at least* two to three people in your life who spring to mind for each category. More is good! This is the foundation of your community of hope.

It's useful to include people you find difficult. They represent a future where you'll definitely have to get on with folks you disagree with. So, pick people you can imagine working alongside (maybe not your nemesis just yet!).

For "everyone else," choose people you look up to in your own community and in wider society.

2. What qualities are available to you with this pool of people? For example:

Friends: Sha'Carri—Patience, quick wits.
Difficult people: Mark—Intelligence, strong-willed.
Everyone else: LeBron James—Reliability, great leader.

3. You are part of this community that represents the best of your circle and the best of what humanity has to offer.

Note all the qualities *you* bring to the party. For example, *determination, empathy.*

4. Finally, name your community. It's like naming a band. Find something you all stand for or that captures your vibe.

Mine (this week) would be *The Dreamlords . . .*

Keep these notes about your community of hope for when you might need them.

Cultivating Peace Inside

There are many antidotes to the anger that sometimes seems to shape society, our communities, and even our homes. This meditation uses different reflections that can help when we feel overwhelmed by anger about the world or other people. It's good for cultivating some inner peace and making sure we have a strong base to set out from in our own lives.

Strengthening Your Mind

1. You can do this anywhere. Wherever you are, make sure you're physically comfortable. Breathe easy and relax, then let your eyes close. Feel the ground under your feet: You are supported. Whatever your feelings and thoughts today, try to keep a sense of the great sky overhead—there's lots of space for things to change.

   Really try to connect with what you'd wish most for yourself in terms of happiness and peace of mind. Spend some time imagining that.

2. Now, remember when you last felt angry or upset about something that eventually got resolved. No need to dwell on the feelings or relive the scenarios; just reflect that it happened— *then it changed*.

   Some other reflections to try:

   - What happened in my body when I got angry?

   - What was it like to brood over the wrongs done to me?

   - How did I feel when there was a resolution?

3. Here are two antidotes to anger you've already learned:

   - Following your breath into a greater sense of awareness.

   - Developing kindness and compassion for other people, including awareness of their suffering.

   Pick whichever you feel would benefit you most now, and spend a few minutes with your breath or with kindness and compassion. (A bit of each is fine, too.)

   Whenever you notice your mind wandering, come back to the meditation and remind yourself of your own best intentions. This can be surprisingly effective! Use some willpower to support your mind.

4. Another antidote we've practiced is letting go: imagining troubles passing, dissolving like clouds in a blue sky.

   Whatever's going on in your mind, heart, and body right now, try to sit back and not get too caught up with it. Just notice. Like weather, it changes. The sky is still overhead. There is so much space open . . .

5. To end, imagine sitting under the tree with the Buddha, whatever the tree and the Buddha look like to you. No judgment—there's nothing else you have to do. Just sit under the tree and let yourself rest.

Do this for as long as you need.

All the Jewels in the Net

Report sealed: August 27, XXXX

Status: Highly Classified

These papers were discovered at Project Jizo when the base was found deserted. All speculation is discouraged—the official record will show the project as discontinued. We may never know what happened there.

Professor Sorensen's notes, batch 1

This brilliant young research assistant! So many questions, so eager to make an impression. I remember I had their fire once. I predict Mal will be at the forefront of many discoveries . . .

Mal Kya's diary, entry 7

Sometimes I dream of a jewel in the sky above the ice. Then, it's under the ice. Its light seems like magic . . .

Professor Sorensen discourages too much dreaming. When I told her, she said, "Just enough to keep you engaged with your work!"

Can dreams be real?

Sorensen, batch 4

Our experiments to map the energy fields in this place of perfect light, perfect shadows, show astounding promise. But we are missing something vital . . .

We can detect so many stars, but only a tiny fraction of the universe. It is magnificent to count them against the indescribable dark. You can feel how precious they and we are.

Kya, entry 11

I used to be obsessed with answers and facts. I like questions better now. Professor S is very patient. So long as my data's ready on time—and validated!

. . . These readings, they can't be right, surely?

Sorensen, batch 17

Facts are real, but I never trust too much certainty. It is not the scientific way. I love science's challenge to always go deeper, to find better ideas and models.

All that nonsense about fixed beginnings and endings to the universe . . . why should humans put our limited ways of understanding at the center of everything?

Kya, entry 18

For weeks we've been testing, retesting. The data suggests a vast net we can't see that connects everything. Throughout and beyond all space and time . . .

Is there a connection to the jewel in my dreams? That would fulfill all our hopes. I'm not sure if I'm awake or dreaming now.

Sorensen, batch 21

A breakthrough! Mal's intuition was right. What they call "the jewel" connects all points of the net. There are infinite gems, each infinitely reflecting all others.

We both felt great peace when we realized this. Like knowing everything and everyone is a gem, potentially connected and reflecting true equality everywhere across the net . . . it is a great, beautiful mystery!

Kya, entry 21

Tonight we'll go further, try and measure one of the connection points. It's our greatest wish now—to touch the jewel's light and see humankind illuminated . . . we don't know what will happen!

Think Points

Buddhism suggests everything and everyone is interconnected. Everything flows. We sparkle like bubbles in the great stream. We can direct our lives like beams of light . . .

I. Do you think the truth is something *you* could find?

II. In what ways do you feel connected to people and places you don't know?

III. Do you prefer imagining reality as a mystery or a set of facts?

Making an Impact

In Buddhist circles, *posture* usually means setting up your body to be strong, comfortable, and well supported in meditation. It can also have the wider sense of the posture—mental *shape* or *attitude*—you take whenever you act in everyday life.

This chapter is focused on the fundamental idea that you have something positive to offer: to your *inner circle* (family, friends, local community, school) and to your *outer circle* (region, state, country, world).

It's important to set up your "posture" well for that: to take yourself seriously while still keeping a sense of humor and perspective for when, like everyone else, you occasionally screw up. This should help you cultivate an open mind and heart about what it looks like to act and make a contribution.

As with "The Story of You" (page 4), you'll be getting clear about your own values. You'll also be thinking about how you might make an impact on society and how society already impacts you.

1. Start by asking yourself some general questions. Record as many answers as you can, in any way you like:

   - What background values influence your intentions when you act? Such as:

     ‣ *Everyone should be kind, including me.*

     ‣ *You have to look after yourself first or you're no good to anyone.*

     ‣ *Family comes before everything else.*

   - What effect do you think your actions have? To your:

     ‣ *Family*

     ‣ *Friends*

     ‣ *School*

- ‣ *Wider world*

- ‣ *Your own mind*

- Give specific examples, like:

  - ‣ *When I help clean up the house, Dad appreciates it.*

  - ‣ *I sometimes struggle to share, but people say I'm a good friend.*

  - ‣ *School's not somewhere I feel I have a voice. I wish I did!*

  - ‣ *I donate to good causes I believe in, so I know people benefit.*

  - ‣ *I have a hard time with confidence, but I like feeling connected and engaged with stuff.*

  Keep your answers to look at later.

2. What issues do you feel you and your friends and family are most affected by? For example, *racism, climate change, inequality, polarized politics, healthcare, gun violence, money, personal freedoms, etc.*

   - How could you imagine engaging around these issues?

     - ‣ *With your family/friends*

     - ‣ *At school*

     - ‣ *In your local community*

     - ‣ *Nationally*

   - Things like:

     - ‣ *Conducting a family/friend poll about the issue(s)*

     - ‣ *Talking to sympathetic teachers (they exist!)*

     - ‣ *Checking the public library for interest groups or relevant events*

> ‣ *Reading the news more carefully, from different kinds of sources*

3. Write a letter to a school, local, or national newspaper/website about the issue you care most about.

In Buddhism, mindfulness is a whole way of being and acting in the world. Our state of mind affects the way we experience everything, and our behavior does, too. This is why, in meditation, mindfulness always merges with kindness.

In ancient India, the Buddha was around many of the same problems we are today. Bias in favor of one kind of person over another. Discrimination against women and people considered "different" or "lesser" in society. Power struggles that keep countries constantly at war. All of this is part of what drove the Buddha to try and "wake up."

Our ancestors could be as painfully confused as we are! Compassion was the Buddhist response; it is the only alternative to harm and violence that can actually lead to peace—in our own hearts, families, communities, and nations, and across generations.

Connecting through Time

1. You can do this meditation anywhere. Be safe and physically comfortable, stay in touch with your breath, and wish yourself well as you start . . .

First, bring to mind the Indigenous Peoples of wherever you now live. Those who inhabited, and may still inhabit, the place you know, including when it looked very different than it does today. (If you don't know the name[s] of these people, look them up first.)

Imagine a line of connection between them and you, running through the land itself and through the sky. Maybe the line is made of light or feels like a breeze. However you want to imagine it is fine.

2. Now, call to mind all the people who emigrated to where you live, perhaps to escape trouble elsewhere. Again, imagine the same line of connection to them.

   Do the same with your own family's ancestors, imagining generations back. Maybe they were immigrants; maybe they always lived there.

3. Imagine sending your best wishes through time to all of these, in whatever way works.

   It might help to remember our definition of compassion from chapter 1: We can "shake" sympathetically with other people because we know what they go through, because of everything we have in common.

4. Now, imagine the landscape where you live when no one was there yet. In the deep past, without people. Just plants, sea creatures, maybe the dinosaurs!

   Now, imagine it in the far future. What will it look like? Will humans still be here?

   Send your compassion back to the deep past and to the far future: to all life, human or not.

5. When it feels right, bring your meditation to an end.

I Was a Teenage Monk

In our village, becoming a monk was a way out. There wasn't much work, except in the fields. Some liked that, but most had no choice. Everyone was poor. Well, someone owned the fields—I guess he did well.

So, I got lucky: I was a teenage monk for a while. I even wandered with the Buddha for a couple of years. Until something happened that made me change course—come back here to make a difference where I was raised.

My first night in the jungle, I was so scared! A night not sleeping, listening to the howls of monkeys, every rustle nearby a hungry python or tiger stalking me . . . Two years later, I'd learned to calm my mind a bit, sleep better. But I hadn't worked out the other half of the Buddha's magic yet: how to live with kindness.

We'd been called to a place where two tribes were about to go to war, including the Buddha's own people. They were terrified of another conflict that would damage their families for generations. As my father says, the only winners are the ones who make the arrows.

It was amazing to watch the Buddha work: listening patiently, asking good questions about what each side valued most. Of course, it was the same—not the dumb land they were fighting over, but the lives of their children, their friends. Eventually, everyone stopped posturing and backed down. It was fragile, but it was peace.

We were getting ready to leave when the Buddha noticed one of our usual crew was missing. Turns out, he was sick and lying alone in a hut nearby. The Buddha asked why no one was looking after him. Someone said, "Oh, he's not been any help packing up camp. When he's better, I'm sure he'll catch up." You should have seen the Buddha's face. Not angry, but a sort of stern care I've only seen a few times and don't think I'll ever forget.

A few of us walked to the hut. The poor guy was really weak. He had diarrhea and needed cleaning, had no water and no company.

The Buddha washed him so carefully, without a big fuss or show, talking with him quietly the whole time. I embarrassedly tidied the hut and made sure he had what he needed. Then, we delayed leaving for a few more days until the man was well enough to come with us.

It was as we finally left that it hit me. Stopping a war, looking after someone who needs it—they are just the same. I returned home not long after that. My daughters will know a different world.

Think Points

Small things turn into big things if you let them. It works both ways: neglect to hate, care to peace. Make your choice every day.

I. In terms of life opportunities, do you think you have it better or worse than your parents' generation? Talk to them, or someone their age, about it.

II. Is a world without war possible, or is that just a dream?

III. What could you do to show more care at home?

Buddhist Detective Club

In chapter 3, we investigated a major Buddhist teaching, the *Noble Eightfold Path* (page 90), identifying which of the stages were relevant to our minds.

Here, we'll consider how all eight stages apply to your whole life as you engage with the world. You can think of them as a sequence of steps on a path. You can also imagine them together like parts of a growing, changing tree: trunk, branches, twigs, and leaves, all interconnected.

At the end of this exercise, you're going to do some Buddhist detective work. Good luck!

1. Take in the remixed version of the stages below. They're arranged differently from last time (see page 78), under the headings of ethics, meditation, and wisdom:

Ethics

   i.   *Action: Causing no harm*

   ii.   *Speech: Speaking truthfully, kindly, harmoniously*

   iii.   *Livelihood: Earning money in a way that doesn't involve harm or exploitation*

Meditation

   iv.   *Mindfulness: Remembering that everything changes and to stay in the present*

   v.   *Effort: Putting time and energy into worthwhile things*

   vi.   *Concentration: Cultivating deeper awareness and positive mental states*

Wisdom

   vii.   *Understanding: Knowing that everything's interconnected, nothing lasts forever, and actions have consequences*

   viii.   *Intention: Being clear about how you want to live*

2. Take a look again at your own freestyle notes from last time around some of the stages. Now, fill in the gaps—the bits that aren't mainly to do with your mind. Like this:

Action: *All my behavior. Is thinking an action, though? Speaking is . . . These all overlap!*

Speech: *I have a bit of a motormouth!*
I'm shy and don't find it easy to speak up for myself.

Livelihood: *My summer job didn't pay well—just tips, really. Is serving meat harmful?*

Effort: *I find it hard to motivate myself sometimes. I'm not lazy. I just get bored.*

When you're done, arrange *all the stages* you've worked on both times into an order that makes sense to you as a complete path. Think about why you chose that order.

3. Go interview *at least three* people you trust about this path in their own life. You can choose any stage(s). Maybe some friends will join you?

Here are some sample questions:

Livelihood: *How satisfied are you with your work? Do you think it's ethical? What were your ambitions when you were my age? What's your relationship to money like?*

Concentration: *When you were younger, did you find school easy, or was it hard to focus? Has that changed in your life since?*

Speech: *What's the best advice anyone's ever given you?*

Your life is part of a much bigger universe! Buddhism teaches that you can feel great freedom of heart when you take on this perspective, realizing that it applies to everyone. It can help you become more thoughtful, empathetic, and compassionate, which makes a real difference in the world.

In this meditation, we'll reflect on the natural elements: *earth, water, fire, and air.* You can do the meditation anywhere, but if you can be outside, it may help you get a stronger sense of the elements in the world.

Becoming the Elements

1. Take a few deep breaths, close your eyes, and then breathe easy and try to relax any tension you can feel. Take in any sounds, the feeling of the breeze or air, any sense of light, anything you can smell, or any lingering taste in your mouth.

   From this place of awareness, send yourself some good wishes. Blow yourself a kiss! Whatever else is going on, you can be proud of trying out this meditation.

2. Feel the ground or earth beneath you. Feel, too, the support of your chair or seat.

   As you breathe, think of the forms of earth elements you know: *soil, rocks, sand, asteroids, diamonds* . . .

   Now, think of all the qualities you associate with the earth: *solid, deep, powerful, soft, hard, shifting* . . .

   And reflect that your body is also made of solid stuff like the earth: *bone, muscle, poop, teeth, spine, skull* . . .

   The solid elements in your body share the same nature as elements that make the stars.

   Now, we're going to follow the same process of reflection for each of the other elements.

3. Water:

The ocean, rivers, streams, ice, rain . . .
Liquid, flowing, wet, soft, strong, hot, cold, deep . . .
Blood, urine, saliva, snot, sweat, tears . . .

The watery elements in your body share the same nature as elements that make the stars.

4. Fire:

The sun, wildfires, matches, grills, embers . . .
Hot, warm, exciting, dangerous, healing, comforting . . .
Body heat, warmth, cold (absence of heat), chills, fever . . .

The elements of heat in your body share the same nature as elements that make the stars.

5. Air:

Wind, humidity, breezes, air-conditioning . . .
Soft, cooling, strong, cold, warm, pleasant, stormy . . .
Breath, farts (!), belches, yawns . . .

The airy elements in your body share the same nature as elements that make the stars.

When you're done, sit in the open space for a while, letting yourself be like the stars.

STORY

Ashes into Gold

Did I dream that life? So long ago. Let me tell you what happened to her. Kisa, *the frail one*—how she grew into her strength.

I had lost my parents. At 16, I wandered where I could be safe, keeping to public places, which is how I found myself in the market one day, looking for scraps of kindness, scraps of food.

A young man was seated on the ground, surrounded by piles of ashes spread on fine rugs, as if he were selling the finest trinkets in

India. That made me smile. The sheer cheek of him! I crouched down, gathered a handful of ashes in my hand, and said pleasantly, "Sir, this is indeed some beautiful gold dust."

He looked delighted. "Ah, someone else can see it! Your powers must be great."

And with that we were bound together. Until, that is, I lost all my gold. Until I was, for a while, made of ashes.

A terrible plague swept through the city, stole our newborn son. My mind went with him. I had survived being orphaned, survived the violence of the streets. I could not survive the scorn of my husband's family: They blamed me.

Picking up my son's body, still warm with fever in my arms, I ran from their house, never to return.

I asked everyone for a doctor. Most backed away, horrified at my burden. But a kind man said: "There is one who might be able to help you." And he walked with me to a garden at the edge of town.

The Stranger was there. She listened so carefully as I begged for the right medicine. Then, when I had exhausted myself, she spoke:

"We can save your son, if you will help me. Go into the city and bring back a mustard seed. Just one, but it must come from a home where nobody has lost a loved one—not a single child, parent, family member, or dear friend."

I ran and ran, never letting go of my boy. The dark whirled around me. Everywhere I went I asked at houses lit up like hope, but always this: a seed offered freely, then a sad shake of the head when I asked about their losses.

I saw the Stranger's face in my mind, heard her voice of calm and kindness. Finally, after the full night of pain, some understanding began to dawn on me: *Everyone has tears; everyone has lost someone.*

In the garden, new friends helped me bury my son. I held the dirt of the earth in my hands as I cried for him, let it sift freely through my fingers like gold dust onto the small square of green.

My heart's strength is all for others now, my life an offering of ashes and gold.

Think Points

Sometimes it's hard to let go of what we love. Our sadness can paralyze us; it's understandable. Everybody needs help to move past grief and back into the world . . .

I. Are you able to talk about feelings of sadness with anyone? Who? If not, would you like to? Why or why not?

II. What is your "gold"—your greatest strength?

ACTIVITY

Time Traveler

Growing up, I was obsessed with a TV show called *Doctor Who*, about a traveler who moved through space and time in a mysterious blue box. I loved the idea of being able to go anywhere and meet anyone who ever existed—or would exist.

Unlike some explorers, the Doctor lived by the belief that you should try to do as little harm as possible when encountering different societies, and hold deep respect for other cultures and ways of life. Which seems pretty Buddhist to me!

When Buddhists say it's good to stay in the present, that doesn't mean the past and future don't matter. We don't want to get too attached to what *could* happen—that leads to disappointment and unhappiness if things don't work out as we hope, or unnecessary worrying when our fears don't actually come true. And we shouldn't try to undo what's already happened—that's impossible and can lead to unresolved regrets. We can still learn lessons from the past and imagine a better future for everyone.

So, if you could travel through time . . .

1. What would your time machine look like? Describe, draw, design, or record it. *(It's fine if it looks like one from a story.)*

2. Pick a time period for both past and future, and explain why you'd go there. For example:
   Prehistoric: I want to see dinosaurs.
   16th century: I want to show Leonardo da Vinci an iPhone.
   23rd century: I want to know if we survive climate change.
   45th century: How far have we traveled across galaxies?

3. Okay, some questions about your travel to the past:

   - Which historical figure would you ask for advice about your future life?

   - If you could meet a younger version of yourself, what age would you choose and why?

   - What advice would you give a younger version of yourself?

   - You can change one thing about your own past: What is it? What would the consequences be?

4. Now, some questions about your time in the future:

   - Which friend(s) and/or family member(s) would you take with you?

   - What will future you be like in 20 years?

   - What issue do you care most strongly about in the future (such as racism, gender equality, government, etc.)?

   - When you think about that issue, what will the world be like in 10 years, 50 years, 100 years, 500 years?

5. If you had to choose *only* the past or future, which would you visit and why? Would you come back, or would you stay?

Your Part in a Better Future

Buddhism isn't an escape from society—it offers an ideal you can carry in your heart and put into practice as you move *through* society. But life has scary things in it, so it's normal to find it hard sometimes and feel depressed. We all need support to avoid getting too down about our place or future in the world. The images and reflections in this meditation can help.

If we cultivate generosity and kindness in our behavior, the effects will ripple out and make a difference in other people's lives. That's how we *really* change society: by becoming an example of how we wish the world would be.

Shadows and Light

1. You can do this anywhere. Close your eyes and try to let go of any tensions from your day. This is a safe space: You're allowed to be at ease.

   Whatever you're holding, wish yourself well. You can use words or your imagination. You can also think of a good friend you trust and just imagine them with you, encouraging and supporting you.

2. Think of someone you know who's a mentor or role model, with qualities and a perspective on life you admire.

   Reflect on what inspires you about them. And imagine them offering those qualities to you as a gift. Perhaps they pass them to you like a physical object. Perhaps they send them to you as a ray of light. However you imagine this is fine.

3. Now, think of someone you dislike or disagree with. Maybe it's around politics, sports, or something about the way they live.

   Imagine you are just giving them your full attention, listening to them without any argument or judgment.

They probably feel sad and lonely sometimes. You know that feeling, too.

4. Everyone carries some sadness with them. Working with our breath, we can take in a sense of humanity's challenges without having to be responsible for them or trying to fix them.

As you breathe in, imagine the world's troubles as shadows. Shadows cast by fears and sadnesses in people's lives.

As you breathe out, imagine sending your love, and the best qualities of you, your friend, and your mentor, into the shadows like light.

Try and include a sense of both the people you do and don't like. Spend a few minutes doing this, gently and with patience: light into the shadows.

When you're ready, finish meditating by letting go of any effort. Just sit for a minute more, breathing and relaxing.

STORY

Letting Go of the Raft

Maya felt panicked, as if she was drowning. Last week of senior year, the night before prom. Ten months building up to this supposedly huge change—and now what?

Only hours ago, she'd felt fine; excited, even. She'd been in one of the classes she actually liked—global studies—and they'd been discussing the story of the Buddha with Mr. Kondan.

"Good luck, everyone!" he'd called as they left his classroom for the last time, some off to summer jobs, some to vacation, then college or straight to full-time work.

Maya knew what she was supposed to be doing next. She just wasn't sure it was what she wanted. The thought of more school depressed her! She longed to head off somewhere, anywhere—totally vanish. Maybe drive cross-country and reemerge in a year as someone different, someone more exotic.

She could hear the sounds of their neighborhood through the window. A bottle breaking, a baby crying hard, dogs freaking out. Her dad was at the factory, late shift, but he'd be home soon.

Maya chewed her lip. She always did that when she thought about her mom. What had she been like?

"Come on, Maya!" she said out loud, and distracted herself with her notebook. She loved the tatty, dog-eared cover: black with the white elephant sticker on the front. Only a few more blank pages.

It fell open at her entries from that afternoon.

Why did that guy say no to the Buddha?

She remembered the teacher's challenge when she'd asked him this. "Why does it matter, Maya?'

She had answered too fiercely: "Because I need to know how to go on!

"I mean, that first guy the Buddha meets? He's not impressed. And he has a point, right? It *sounds* great, but really it's just another dumb religion . . ."

Someone else had spoken up then: "Well, it's the only religion that basically makes itself disappear . . ."

Now she read two notes of her own about the conversation, written in her fast, furious hand:

Buddhism sees itself like a raft for crossing a fast-moving river. It just helps you get from one shore to the other safely. It's not something you do for its own sake. You wouldn't carry the raft on your head afterward!

The Buddha isn't interested in being conventional. Only in living the truth, understanding whatever sets us free. The rest is up to you . . .

Maya felt relieved. Whatever she did next, it was as if the wide world suddenly beckoned her.

At the end, Mr. Kondan had surprised them all:

"For what it's worth, people, I trust you."

She smiled now, and said into the night: "Yeah. I think I've got it now."

Think Points

Buddhism = deep awareness + deep kindness. The rest really is up to you. Choose your stories, then go and live inside them.

I. How would you sum up Buddhism yourself?

II. If someone told you they'd discovered the truth, how would you assess that?

III. When you think about meeting the world as an adult, what's your number one question?

ACTIVITY

Invent Your Own Religion

The Buddha had this to say about any vision or experience of reality that opens up a genuine path to truth and happiness:

"Just as the great ocean has one taste—the taste of salt—the truth should have one taste: the taste of freedom."

But as you might have noticed, what freedom actually *means* to people—in different cultures, societies, even within a single country—is often an issue. Still, it's amazing to have a philosophy/religion/ way of life that's interested in you finding out the answers for yourself, rather than just "believing" something you're told.

You've just read this book on Buddhism, explored the open world of its stories, activities, and meditations. How would *you* explain the path to wisdom to someone? For our final activity, we're going to play *Invent Your Own Religion*.

1. You can do this on your own. You can also take it on with friends—do it as a group and see what you all come up with at the end when you pool your answers.

2. Sit in silence for a few minutes first.

3. What would a spiritual community or religion look like for you?
   Doing this on your own? Capture your thoughts and answers any way you like. Doing it as a group? Take turns speaking, or note things privately and share them after.
   Here are some more detailed questions you can ask (with sample answers you can riff on):

   ### Who would get to be in it and why?

   - *Whoever wants to be: open to everyone. Obviously!*

   - *Only people who agree with me about social justice! Harmony matters . . .*

   ### What personal qualities would people develop as a result of your religion?

   - *Kindness and patience.*

   - *They'd be strong and know what they believe.*

   ### What kind of practices would they do, together and as individuals? (Choose ones you respond to or benefit from.)
   Meditation, prayer, singing, chanting, retreats, time alone, sharing feelings and experiences, study, having fun.

What would its essential values and teachings be?

- *Kindness is central.*

- *A strong sense of rules and discipline matter.*

- *Give to others what they need to be happy (not necessarily what you want).*

What sources would it come from?

Traditional religion, Indigenous cultures, art, science, literature, gaming, online memes.

Would it have a leader or central teacher?

- *Yes, me!*

- *Definitely not!*

- *Let leadership develop organically within the community.*

What other questions could you ask?

Keep your answers, and add to them over time as your experience changes.

MEDITATION

Setting Out into the World

It seems right to finish this book with a meditation inspired by the last thing the Buddha did before setting out into the world from under the tree.

This is something you can do anytime, anywhere. And if you can manage it, try meditating under an actual tree sometime!

Sitting, Being, Standing, Leaving

1. Let your eyes close and set yourself comfortably to meditate.

   Imagine other people with you, maybe from your relationship mandala (page 26) or community of hope (page 98). They're just sitting with you, relaxing, breathing. You're not on your own with any of this.

2. Get a sense of your physical body as your breath rises and falls naturally. Imagine that your breath fills the whole inside of your body as you breathe in, and the space around it as you breathe out.
   Now for a thought experiment:

   - What if your body was made only of feelings? What shape would it have?
     Loose and expansive? Compact and firm? Something else?

   - What if your body was made only of thoughts? What form would it take then?
     Let your imagination be free to roam with this.

   - Wish/imagine yourself well in each of your three "bodies":
     May I be happy in all my aspects!

3. Imagine a scene with these elements:

   - A clear blue sky *(day or night)*

   - The green or dusty earth *(supporting you)*

   - A tree *(any kind you wish)*

   - A comfortable seat under or near it for you *(could be made of grass, could be your wheelchair)*

   - The Buddha with any form, color, shape, gender/non-gender you like *(the Buddha is bigger than any single identity)*

   Can you "feel" the scene in your mind? (Don't worry if it's not a visual experience for you.)

4. Play a bit! Try imagining *yourself* as the Buddha under the tree. Or sitting in front of the Buddha under the tree. What's the tree like? Its species, season, leaves, bark, height, and width around . . .

5. Before heading out to teach, it's said the Buddha turned to the tree and bowed in thanks for its shade and shelter from the sun and rain.

Stand up if you're able, or sit in your chair as you might for a more formal meeting than usual. Then—either in your mind or as a physical act—make a little bow to your imagined tree.

Feel it behind you as you set out into the world to make your contribution, to make a difference.

The Road Ahead

Thanks for joining me on this voyage around Buddhism—it's been awesome!

I hope everything we've covered will give you a lot of confidence in the many qualities you already have, and help you develop the kinds of strengths you want to, for whatever comes next in this magical human life. As a person in your own right, friend, family member, citizen in society.

Remember, whatever path you take, you'll be choosing strengths *and* limitations, because every way of life, every community we join, is made with other human beings, and we're all still learning how! You'll have to remake your choices every so often through the years, and that's a good thing.

I hope you've found some of what Buddhism has to say fascinating. If you want to explore more, there are some brilliant resources after this chapter. Either way, it's encouraging to encounter such a long history of human curiosity, imagination, confusion, mistakes, change, awareness, clarity, kindness, and love.

Please take your life seriously in all the best ways! Cultivate a truly open mind, let your body and heart feel free, and trust what you can contribute to the world—by yourself and with others.

May you always find courage; may you always know peace.

Resources

Websites

Access to Insight (accesstoinsight.org)—The stories in this book are based around classic Buddhist tales, teachings, and texts. This site offers free access to many of the originals.

The Buddhist Centre Online (TheBuddhistCentre.com/live)—Daily live meditations and regular Buddhist events you can take part in from home.

Free Buddhist Audio (FreeBuddhistAudio.com)—A collection of 5,000+ audio talks on Buddhism and guided meditations—all free!

Insight Timer app and website (InsightTimer.com)—A huge collection of guided meditations.

Wildmind (WildMind.org)—A great resource for going deeper with meditation.

Books

Check out your local public library for free access to Buddhist books!

Awakening Together: The Spiritual Practice of Inclusivity and Community by Larry Yang—An excellent guide to exploring how Buddhism can offer a sense of freedom for all peoples and communities.

Change Your Mind: A Practical Guide to Buddhist Meditation by Paramananda—One of most accessible, in-depth introductions to meditation.

The Dhammapada: A New Translation of the Buddhist Classic with Annotations, translated by Gil Fronsdal—One of the best-known collections of the Buddha's teachings. There are *lots* of free versions online and different translations.

Living Well with Pain and Illness: The Mindful Way to Free Yourself from Suffering by Vidyamala Burch—Vidyamala has pioneered mindful approaches to dealing with stress, chronic pain, and illness. She's amazing!

Who Is the Buddha? by Sangharakshita—The first book on Buddhism I read. Lots to think about and wrestle with! A great introduction to the Buddha's teaching.

Podcasts

The Buddhist Centre Podcast (AudioBoom.com/channels/4929068)—Conversations among diverse voices from around the world. Often presented by me!

Dharmabytes (FreeBuddhistAudio.com/podcasts)—A podcast from Free Buddhist Audio. Short, inspiring clips of Buddhist wisdom three times a week.

References

Chapter 1

Access to Insight, ed. "A Sketch of the Buddha's Life: Readings from the Pali Canon." Access to Insight (BCBS Edition). November 30, 2013. accesstoinsight.org/ptf/buddha.html.

Berzin, Alexander. "Overdependence on the Spiritual Teacher." StudyBuddhism.com. Accessed July 30, 2021. StudyBuddhism .com/en/advanced-studies/lam-rim/student-teacher-relationship /unhealthy-relationships-with-spiritual-teachers/overdependence -on-the-spiritual-teacher.

Bhikkhu, Ṭhānissaro, trans. "To Anuruddha: Anuruddha Sutta." DhammaTalks.org. Accessed July 30, 2021. DhammaTalks.org /suttas/AN/AN8_30.html.

Cowell, E. B. "Introduction." In *The Buddha-karita of Asvaghosha*. Oxford: Clarendon Press, 1894. Accessed July 30, 2021. Sacred-Texts.com/bud/sbe49/sbe4902.htm.

Decleer, Hubert. "Atisha's Arrival in Nepal." Accessed July 30, 2021. Buddhim.20m.com/8-1.htm.

Feldman, Christina and Chris Cullen. "An Appropriate Response." *Tricycle*. May 10, 2020. Tricycle.org/trikedaily/universal-empathy.

Garmon, Meredith. "Blue Cliff Record 1, Book of Serenity 2." *Boundless Way Zen Westchester* (blog). November 10, 2015. Bowzwestchester.org/2015/11/nov-9-15.html.

Heyman, Jivana. "Making Meditation Accessible." Yoga International. Accessed July 30, 2021. YogaInternational.com/article/view /making-meditation-accessible.

Johnston, E. H., trans. *Ashvaghosha's Buddhacarita or Acts of the Buddha*. Delhi: Motilal Banarsidass Publications, 2015.

Ratnaprabha, trans. "The Karaniya Metta Sutta in Pali and English (PDF Version)." November 1, 2013. TheBuddhistCentre.com /features/urban-retreat-2013-blazing-sun/metta-sutta-pali-and -english-pdf.

Sangharakshita. *What Is Dharma?: The Essential Teachings of the Buddha.* Birmingham, UK: Windhorse Publications, 1998.

Thera, Soma, trans. "Kalama Sutta: The Buddha's Charter of Free Inquiry." Access to Insight (BCBS Edition). November 30, 2013. accesstoinsight.org/lib/authors/soma/wheel008.html.

YJ Editors. "A Beginner's Guide to Pranayama." *Yoga Journal*. March 25, 2021. YogaJournal.com/practice/beginners/how-to/pranayama.

Chapter 2

Bhikkhu, Thānissaro, trans. "Anapanasati Sutta: Mindfulness of Breathing." Access to Insight (BCBS Edition). November 30, 2013. accesstoinsight.org/tipitaka/mn/mn.118.than.html.

Bhikkhu, Thānissaro, trans. "Chiggala Sutta: The Hole." Access to Insight (BCBS Edition). July 1, 2010. accesstoinsight.org/tipitaka /sn/sn56/sn56.048.than.html.

Bhikkhu, Thānissaro, trans. "Cula-Malunkyovada Sutta: The Shorter Instructions to Malunkya." Access to Insight (BCBS Edition). November 30, 2013. accesstoinsight.org/tipitaka/mn/mn.063 .than.html.

Bhikkhu, Thānissaro, trans. "Sallatha Sutta: The Arrow." Access to Insight (BCBS Edition). November 30, 2013. accesstoinsight.org /tipitaka/sn/sn36/sn36.006.than.html.

Cleary, Thomas J. and J. C., trans. *The Blue Cliff Record.* Boston: Shambhala Publications, 1977.

Dogen. "Instructions for the Cook (*Tenzo kyôkun*)." Translated by Griffith Foulk. TheZenSite.com. Accessed August 11, 2021. TheZenSite.com/ZenTeachings/Dogen_Teachings/Instructions _for_the_cook.html.

Gampopa. *The Jewel Ornament of Liberation: The Wish-Fulfilling Gem of the Noble Teachings*. Translated by Khenpo Konchog Gyaltsen Rinpoche. Ithaca, NY: Snow Lion Publications, 1998.

Hecker, Hellmuth. "Angulimala: A Murderer's Road to Sainthood." Access to Insight (BCBS Edition). November 30, 2013. Access ToInsight.org/lib/authors/hecker/wheel312.html.

Vessantara. *A Guide to the Buddhas*. Birmingham, UK: Windhorse Publications, 1993.

Chapter 3

Access to Insight, ed. "Khanda Vagga—The Section on the Aggregates." In *Samyutta Nikaya: The Grouped Discourses*. Access to Insight (BCBS Edition). December 21, 2013. accesstoinsight.org /tipitaka/sn/index.html#khandha.

Bhikkhu, Thānissaro, trans. "Dhammacakkappavattana Sutta: Setting the Wheel of Dhamma in Motion." Access to Insight (BCBS Edition). November 30, 2013. accesstoinsight.org/tipitaka/sn/sn56 /sn56.011.than.html.

Bhikkhu, Thānissaro, trans. "Maha-nidana Sutta: The Great Causes Discourse." Access to Insight (BCBS Edition). November 30, 2013. accesstoinsight.org/tipitaka/dn/dn.15.0.than.html.

Bhikkhu, Thānissaro, trans. "Nagara Sutta: The City." Access to Insight (BCBS Edition). November 30, 2013. accesstoinsight.org /tipitaka/sn/sn12/sn12.065.than.html.

Bhikkhu, Thānissaro, trans. "Samaññaphala Sutta: The Fruits of the Contemplative Life." Access to Insight (BCBS Edition). November 30, 2013. accesstoinsight.org/tipitaka/dn/dn.02.0.than.html.

Bhikkhu, Thānissaro, trans. "Tittha Sutta: Sectarians (1)." Access to Insight (BCBS Edition). September 3, 2012. accesstoinsight.org /tipitaka/kn/ud/ud.6.04.than.html.

Bhikkhu, Thānissaro, trans. "Udāna | Exclamations." DhammaTalks .org. Accessed August 23, 2021. DhammaTalks.org/suttas/KN/Ud /index_Ud.html.

Bodhi, Bhikkhu, trans. "Upanisa Sutta: Discourse on Supporting Conditions." Access to Insight (BCBS Edition). June 13, 2010. accesstoinsight.org/tipitaka/sn/sn12/sn12.023.bodh.html.

"Bodhicaryāvatāra Series." Lotsawa House. Accessed August 23, 2021. LotsawaHouse.org/topics/bodhicharyavatara.

Candasiri, Ajahn. "The Buddha's Advice to Meghiya (Meghiya Sutta)." Quang Duc. March 2, 2011. QuangDuc.com/a32848/the-buddha -s-advice-to-meghiya.

Carus, Paul, ed. "Kassapa, The Fire-Worshiper." In *Buddha, the Gospel.* Chicago: The Open Court Publishing Company,1894. Accessed August 23, 2021. Sacred-Texts.com/bud/btg/btg20.htm.

Cleary, Thomas J. and J. C., trans. *The Blue Cliff Record.* Boston: Shambhala Publications, 1977.

Jayarava. "A Footnote to Sangharakshita's 'A Survey of Buddhism.'" Jayarava.org. May 2004. Jayarava.org/footnote.html.

Keown, Damien. *Buddhism: A Very Short Introduction,* New York: Oxford University Press, 1996.

Sangharakshita. "Lecture 184: The 24 Nidanas." Accessed August 23, 2021. FreeBuddhistAudio.com/texts/lecturetexts/184_The_24 _Nidanas.pdf.

Sangharakshita. *A Survey of Buddhism.* Cambridge, UK: Windhorse Publications, 2014.

Sujato. "The Date of the Flower Sermon." *Sujato's Blog* (blog). May 22, 2011. Sujato.wordpress.com/2011/05/22/the-date-of -the-flower-sermon.

Thera, Ñanamoli, trans. "Adittapariyaya Sutta: The Fire Sermon." Access to Insight (BCBS Edition). November 30, 2013. accesstoinsight.org/tipitaka/sn/sn35/sn35.028.nymo.html.

Chapter 4

Bhikkhu, Thānissaro, trans. "Alagaddupama Sutta: The Water-Snake Simile." Access to Insight (BCBS Edition). December 17, 2013. accesstoinsight.org/tipitaka/mn/mn.022.than.html.

Bhikkhu, Thānissaro, trans. "Bhaya-bherava Sutta: Fear & Terror." Access to Insight (BCBS Edition). November 30, 2013. Access ToInsight.org/tipitaka/mn/mn.004.than.html.

Bhikkhu, Thānissaro. "Kucchivikara-vatthu: The Monk with Dysentary." Access to Insight (BCBS Edition). November 30, 2013. Access ToInsight.org/tipitaka/vin/mv/mv.08.26.01-08.than.html.

Bhikkhu, Thānissaro, trans. "Muccalinda Sutta: About Muccalinda." Access to Insight (BCBS Edition). August 30, 2012. Access ToInsight.org/tipitaka/kn/ud/ud.2.01.than.html.

Bhikkhu, Thānissaro, trans. "Nagara Sutta: The City." Access to Insight (BCBS Edition). November 30, 2013. accesstoinsight.org /tipitaka/sn/sn12/sn12.065.than.html.

Cook, Francis H. *Hua-Yen Buddhism: The Jewel Net of Indra.* State College, PA: The Pennsylvania State University Press, 1977.

Dharmachakra Translation Committee, trans. "Lalitavistara." Last modified 2021. read.84000.co/translation/toh95.html.

Francis, H.T., trans. "No. 536: Kunala-Jakata." Internet Sacred Text Archive. Accessed September 3, 2021. Sacred-Texts.com/bud/j5 /j5029.htm.

Geshe Chekawa Yeshe Dorje. "Seven Points of Mind Training." Translated by Adam Pearcey. Lotsawa House. Accessed September 3, 2021. LotsawaHouse.org/tibetan-masters/geshe-chekhawa -yeshe-dorje/seven-points-mind-training.

Hecker, Hellmuth. "Buddhist Women at the Time of The Buddha." Translated by Sister Khema. Access to Insight (BCBS Edition). November 30, 2013. accesstoinsight.org/lib/authors/hecker /wheel292.html#kisa.

Ireland, John D., trans. "Uposatha Sutta: The Observance Day." Access to Insight (BCBS Edition). June 13, 2010. accesstoinsight .org/tipitaka/kn/ud/ud.5.05.irel.html.

Kabat-Zinn, Jon. "Indra's Net at Work: The Mainstreaming of Dharma Practice in Society." In *The Psychology of Awakening: Buddhism, Science, and Our Day-to-Day Lives.* Gay Watson, Stephen Batchelor, and Guy Claxton, eds. Newburyport, MA: Red Wheel/Weiser, 2000.

Sangharakshita. "The Buddha's Noble Eightfold Path" (lecture series). Free Buddhist Audio. 1968. Accessed September 3, 2021. FreeBuddhistAudio.com/series/details?num=X07.

Sangharakshita. "Looking at the Bodhi Tree" (lecture). Free Buddhist Audio. 1999. Accessed September 3, 2021. FreeBuddhistAudio .com/audio/details?num=192.

Spagnoli, Maria. "Searching for the Origin of the 'bhūmisparśa-mudrā.'" *East and West* 55, no. 1/4 (December 2005): 329–44. JSTOR.org /stable/29757652.

Trungpa, Chögyam. *Training the Mind and Cultivating Loving-Kindness.* Boston: Shambala Publications, 1993.

Watters, Thomas. *On Yuan Chwang's Travels in India.* London: Royal Asiatic Society, 1905.

Index

Acknowledgments

Thanks to Laura Horwood-Benton for all her creative, thoughtful input on my drafts, first to last. This is a better book because of her patient support. Thanks also to my excellent and kindly editors, John Paul Makowski and Patty Consolazio. And to Matt Buonaguro and all at Callisto Media.

"Getting Out of the Story" is partly adapted from conversations with my friend Shraddhavani, with appreciation for her wisdom!

Finally, thanks to all my teachers, and to everyone who has helped me on the path.

About the Author

 **Candradasa** was born in Canada and grew up in Scotland. He was ordained as a member of the Triratna Buddhist Order in 2001 and is the director of Dharmachakra, a nonprofit providing free access to resources on Buddhism, meditation, mindfulness, and life.

Candradasa lives in Portsmouth, New Hampshire, where he is a cofounder and teacher at the Portsmouth Buddhist Center. His writing has been published in journals and online (sometimes under his given name, Michael Venditozzi). He was nominated for the 2020 Pushcart Prize for poetry.

Website: Rascal.press

Instagram: Instagram.com/rascalpress

Twitter: Twitter.com/rascalpress

CPSIA information can be obtained
at www.ICGtesting.com
Printed in the USA
JSHW041916120222
22846JS00003B/6

9 781638 781103